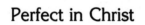

Perfect in Christ

Perfect in Christ

The Mediation of Christ
in the Writings of Ellen G. White

Helmut Ott

REVIEW AND HERALD PUBLISHING ASSOCIATION
Washington, DC 20039-0555
Hagerstown, MD 21740

This book was
Edited by Gerald Wheeler
Designed by Richard Steadham
Type set: 11/12 Baskerville

PRINTED IN U.S.A.

The author assumes full responsibility for the accuracy
of all facts and quotations cited in this book.

Review and Herald Cataloging Service

Ott, Helmut, 1935-
    Perfect in Christ: The mediation of Christ in the writings of

    Ellen G. White.

    1. Sanctification. 2. Sanctuary. 3. Perfection. I. Title.
        234

ISBN 0-8280-0396-3

Contents

Introduction

One of the most significant teachings of the Seventh-day Adventist Church is what is usually referred to as the heavenly sanctuary. The doctrine is generally divided into two distinct yet interrelated parts, namely the so-called investigative judgment and the mediatorial ministry of Christ. The former deals with what Christ, in His role as judge, does to establish the eternal destiny of the dead—how He formalizes the righteous standing of those who during their lifetime were willing to cooperate with God's redemptive activity on their behalf. The latter concerns itself with what Christ, as man's representative and advocate, does to establish the eternal destiny of the living—how He secures the salvation of those who live depending on the Saviour's atoning death, redemptive victory, and all-sufficient righteousness for a right standing with God.

From the beginning Adventists perceived this doctrine to be both important and timely. By pointing to Jesus as the only rightful and effective mediator between God and man, it exposed a false system of mediation that had crept into the Christian church. The human system of priesthood that for centuries had prevailed in Christendom had arrogated to itself the role and the function that, according to Scripture, belong only to Christ, the heavenly high priest. The concept established the church as another mediator between God and man, another way to find favor with God.

The introduction of the system of priesthood both

7

reflected and perpetuated a change in the church's self-understanding. The apostolic church viewed itself as the fellowship of believers—those who, by responding to the gospel in repentance and faith, had accepted Jesus Christ as their personal Saviour. The early believers had a strongly Christ-centered self-understanding. They saw Jesus as their "righteousness, holiness and redemption," their "life," their "hope," their "all" (1 Cor. 1:30; Col. 3:4; 1 Tim. 1:1; Col. 3:11). To them He was "the reality" (Col. 2:17) of which the believer partakes by faith.

The apostolic Christians knew that they were already "sons of God through faith in Christ Jesus" (Gal. 3:26). Because they were sons, they were also "heirs according to the promise" (verse 29). But they also recognized that most of what the gospel promises does not become a concrete reality for the believer during his present existence. It will be fully realized only in the future, eternal life. In the meantime it is real only in the person of Jesus Christ. Therefore, the only way the believer can have access to the gospel promises is through Christ.

> Once you were alienated from God and were enemies in your minds because of your evil behavior. But now he has reconciled you by Christ's physical body through death *to present you holy in his sight,* without blemish and free from accusation—*if you continue in your faith,* established and firm, not moved from the hope held out in the gospel (Col. 1:21-23). Brothers, I want to remind you of the gospel I preached to you . . . *By this gospel you are saved, if you hold firmly* to the word I preached to you. Otherwise, you have believed in vain (1 Cor. 15:1, 2).

> God has given us eternal life, and this life is in his Son. *He who has the Son has life;* he who does not have the Son of God does not have life (1 John 5:11, 12). We have come to share in Christ *if we hold firmly till the end* the confidence

we had at first (Heb. 3:14). And now, dear children, *continue in him,* so that when he appears we may be confident and unashamed before him at his coming (1 John 2:28). So then, just as you received Christ Jesus as Lord, *continue to live in him,* rooted and built up in him, strengthened in the faith as you were taught, and over-flowing with thankfulness (Col. 2:6, 7).

The early Christians understood that all they were and all they had as sons and daughters of God, they were and they had only because—and for so long as—they remained in Christ by faith. They knew that if they ever lost their hold on Him— and consequently ceased to participate in His redemptive work on their behalf—they would revert to their previous state of lostness and would be subject to the old order of sin, condemnation, and death. It was therefore imperative that they continue living by faith in Christ throughout their lives. That was the only way in which what they now had by faith, as a promise, would become a concrete historical reality for them at the second coming of Jesus.

In time the Christ-centered self-understanding changed, and the church became a hierarchical institution that viewed itself, not as the dependent object of God's grace, but as its sole possessor and dispenser. Thus the church increasingly functioned as the authoritative agency that presumably could either actualize or frustrate a sinner's reconciliation with God. For all practical purposes Jesus was displaced by the church as the "author and perfecter of our faith," the only "source of eternal salvation" (Heb. 12:2; 5:9). Adventists believed a correct understanding of the sanctuary doctrine would play a major role in recapturing the apostolic perceptions and experience. First, it would expose the false systems of mediation that had been established, and reveal the fallacy of depending on any human institution, method, merit, or achievement for a right standing with God.

The sanctuary doctrine also called attention to the true way God has provided in Christ for man's reconciliation with the Father. Christendom had almost completely lost sight of Christ's mediatorial/substitutionary role in heaven. The sanctuary doctrine would bring this dimension to the forefront. It would present Jesus as the living Saviour who, as man's substitute and surety, "stands in the holy of holies, now to appear in the presence of God for us. There He ceases not to present His people moment by moment, complete in Himself" *(Faith and Works,* p. 107).

The fact that the Mediator presents His people complete *in Himself*—that is, by imputing to them His personal merits—clearly indicates that in Christ all sinners have equal access to the Father. Thanks to the Saviour's substitutionary role—first on the cross as atoning sacrifice, and now on the throne as mediating advocate—all true believers stand before God totally forgiven and perfectly righteous in Christ.

Third, by calling the believers' attention away from themselves and their meager accomplishments—their imperfect obedience, uneven growth, and incomplete maturity—and by focusing their attention on Jesus and His redemptive ministry on their behalf, the sanctuary doctrine would remove fear and insecurity and replaced them with peace, assurance, and joy. The following passages from Ellen White's writings bring this out quite clearly:

> The intercession of Christ in our behalf is that of presenting His divine merits in the offering of Himself to the Father as our substitute and surety; for He ascended up on high to make an atonement for our transgressions.

INTRODUCTION

"If any man sin, we have an advocate with the Father, Jesus Christ the righteous: and he is the propitiation for our sins: and not for our's only, but also for the sins of the whole world" (1 John 2:1, 2). "Herein is love, not that we loved God, but that he loved us, and sent his Son to be the propitiation for our sins" (1 John 4:10). "He is able also to save them to the uttermost that come unto God by him, seeing he ever liveth to make intercession for them" (Heb. 7:25). From these scriptures it is evident that it is not God's will that you should be distrustful and torture your soul with the fear that God will not accept you because you are sinful and unworthy. "Draw nigh to God, and he will draw nigh to you" (James 4:8). Present your case before Him, pleading the merits of the blood shed for you upon Calvary's cross *(ibid.,* pp. 105, 106).

We must not trust at all to ourselves or to our good works; but when as erring, sinful beings we come to Christ, we may find rest in His love. God will accept everyone that comes to Him trusting wholly in the merits of a crucified Saviour *(ibid.,* p. 39). We must center our hopes of heaven upon Christ alone, because He is our Substitute and Surety. We have transgressed the law of God, and by the deeds of the law shall no flesh be justified. The best efforts that man in his own strength can make are valueless to meet the holy and just law that he has transgressed; but through faith in Christ he may claim the righteousness of the Son of God as all-sufficient *(ibid.,* p. 93).

Finally, a personal knowledge of the high priestly ministry of Christ in heaven would enable God's people to establish and maintain a saving faith relationship with Him, and to fulfill the role God intended for them. Notice how the following statement expresses this idea:

All need a knowledge for themselves of the position and work of their great High Priest. Otherwise it will be impossible for them to exercise the faith which is essential

11

at this time or to occupy the position which God designs them to fill. . . . The intercession of Christ in man's behalf in the sanctuary above is as essential to the plan of salvation as was His death upon the cross *(The Great Controversy,* pp. 488, 489).

The passage presents two major concepts. First, it underlines the tremendous significance Christ's intercession in man's behalf has for the plan of salvation: it is "as essential . . . as was His death upon the cross." And second, it indicates that we can neither have essential faith nor occupy our God-ordained position unless we have a reliable personal understanding of Jesus as our great High Priest.

The importance of Christ's mediatorial ministry and its implications for our personal Christian experience should have moved us as a church to place it high on our agenda. Unfortunately, that has not been the case. Historically the Adventist community has paid considerably more attention to Christ's role as judge of the dead than to His role as mediator for the living.

The reason for this is not that the former is more important—for that is most definitely not the case—but that it is more controversial. In order to establish some aspects of this phase of the judgment, one must build conceptual bridges, establish textual relationships, draw conclusions, and derive implications that are not as scripturally evident as many would desire them to be. As a result, we have been so intensely occupied with reaching consensus on some details concerning God's judgment of the dead that we have almost totally neglected to concern ourselves with His ongoing work for the redemption of the living.

Predictably, such a one-sided emphasis has had some rather negative side effects. On the one hand, it has distracted us from proclaiming Jesus as the only rightful and effectual mediator between God and man. To tell the world that we cannot base our assurance of salvation either on the earthly church (its role, institutions, and ministry) or on the believer himself (his personal goodness, accomplishments, and merits) but on Jesus and what He is doing for us in heaven has certainly not been one of our foremost concerns. Hence, to the extent that we have failed to make this truth central to our message and mission, we have already failed to "occupy the position which God designs" us to fill.

On the other hand, our one-sided emphasis has prevented us from acquiring a clearer understanding of exactly what Jesus is presently doing on our behalf, and how His ministry should determine the nature and quality of our personal faith relationship with Him. As a result, some ideas have found their way into Adventism that, instead of stressing Jesus as the only source of saving righteousness for fallen man, actually make the believer's own character development and behavior modification the ultimate criteria for his standing with God. Thus the center of attention as well as the hope of salvation have shifted from Jesus and what He does for the believer in heaven to what he experiences in his personal life here on earth—a subtle yet tremendously significant change that contradicts the essence as well as purpose of the sanctuary doctrine.

This brings us to the three major objectives of our present study: first, to restore Christ's high-priestly ministry to the forefront of our attention and refine our understanding of what Jesus, as our representative and advocate with the Father, is presently doing. Second, to enhance our relationship with Christ as our mediator and remind us that His atoning death, redemptive victory, and saving righteousness are the only basis of our acceptance with God, our only hope of salvation.

And third, to provide a fairly systematic and reasonably comprehensive structure to the many teachings we find on this subject in Ellen White's writings.

In the process we will attempt to find the answer her writings provide to at least the following two basic questions: 1. Why is the mediation of Christ considered so important to the plan of salvation? That is, what is Jesus doing as our personal "substitute and surety"—two of her favorite terms—that is so vital to our ultimate salvation? 2. And what response should Christ's mediatorial role elicit from us as believers? What must we do in order to allow the Saviour to carry forward His redemptive work on our behalf to its final and total realization at the second coming of Christ?

I have based this study almost exclusively on Ellen White's writings. As a result, I have presented only enough biblical evidence to show that the concepts derived from her writings harmonize with Scripture, and that we can therefore accept the concepts as reliable. I have two reasons for this approach. First, Ellen White is by far the foremost exponent of the Adventist understanding of Christ's mediatorial ministry and its significance. Second, although she wrote much on the topic —references to it appear almost everywhere in her works—for the most part she was neither systematic nor definitive enough to prevent misunderstanding. Therefore it should come as no surprise that some use portions of her writings to support views that, instead of centering on Christ and His redemptive ministry in heaven, focus primarily on man and his meager accomplishments here on earth.

Should such man-centered ideas become prevalent within Adventism, they would indeed make it "impossible" for us to "exercise the faith which is essential at this time." I have written this book in the hope that, by

INTRODUCTION

aiding our understanding of Christ's mediatorial ministry, it will enable us to recognize and deal with deceptive
views, and move us to establish and maintain a strong
personal faith relationship with Jesus Christ until He
comes.

The study falls into eight general sections: 1. The
mediation of Christ for the believer as an individual
person. 2. The mediation of Christ for the believer's
performance. 3. The mediation of Christ as the only
source of saving righteousness for all. 4. The mediation
of Christ as the only source of saving righteousness until
He returns. 5. The mediation of Christ completed at the
close of probation. 6. Ellen White and a deception
aimed particularly at Adventists. 7. Two groups of
people within the church: those righteous in Christ, and
those unrighteous. 8. Summary and conclusions. The
appendix outlines some basic principles concerning the
use of Ellen White's writings and provides some exam-
ples of ways to deal with passages that at first reading
appear to be in tension with the concepts established in
this book.

I Christ Mediates for the Believer to Present Him—As an Individual Person—Perfectly Righteous to the Father

In this chapter we examine the first basic reason that Ellen White considers the mediatorial ministry of Christ so essential to the plan of salvation. We begin by establishing why the believer must depend on Christ as his personal mediator and representative with the Father. Then we see exactly what, according to our source, Jesus is doing to present the believer perfectly acceptable to God. In the third section we discuss the relationship between the believer's lifelong process of sanctification and his dependence on Christ's mediation for a right standing with God. Finally we examine a few relevant scriptural passages.

1. Why the Believer Depends on Christ's Mediation for a Right Standing With God

The condition of eternal life is now just what it always has been—just what it was in Paradise before the fall of our first parents—perfect obedience to the law of God, perfect righteousness (*Steps to Christ*, p. 62). Apart from Christ we have no merit, no righteousness. Our sinfulness, our weakness, our human imperfection make it impossible that we should appear before God unless we are clothed in Christ's spotless righteousness (*Selected Messages*, book 1, p. 333).

Righteousness without blemish can be obtained only through the imputed righteousness of Christ (Ellen G. White, in *Review and Herald,* Sept. 3, 1901). The guests at the marriage feast were inspected by the king. Only those were accepted who had obeyed his requirements and put on the wedding garment. So it is with the guests at the gospel feast. All must pass the scrutiny of the great King, and only those are received who have put on the robe of Christ's righteousness *(Christ's Object Lessons,* p. 312).

The only way in which [the sinner] can attain to righteousness is through faith. By faith he can bring to God the merits of Christ, and the Lord places the obedience of His Son to the sinner's account. Christ's righteousness is accepted in place of man's failure, and God receives, pardons, justifies, the repentant, believing soul, treats him as though he were righteous, and loves him as He loves His Son. This is how faith is accounted righteousness *(Selected Messages,* book 1, p. 367).

One can hardly read such statements without being impressed by the definite, almost radical nature of both the concepts they contain and the language she used to express them. Notice these important points in them:

1. God requires *perfect righteousness* of those who will inherit eternal life—nothing less will do.

2. Apart from Christ *we have no righteousness, no merit,* on which to provide God a basis to accept us.

3. Our sinfulness, our human imperfection, makes it *impossible* for us to appear before God *unless* we are clothed in Christ's righteousness.

4. We can obtain *righteousness without blemish*—the only righteousness God can approve—*only through the imputed righteousness of Christ.*

5. The king checks all the guests of the gospel feast—those who respond to the invitation and come—to make sure they meet the requirements. *Only those* who

have put on the robe of Christ's righteousness can participate. All the others—regardless of any personal qualifications or moral virtues they might possess—find themselves cast out.

6. God regards Christ's perfect righteousness *in place of* man's failure. *"This is how faith is accounted righteousness."*

Such considerations lead us to conclude that the Christian depends on Christ's mediation because God requires perfect righteousness—something the believer cannot produce. He is a sinner, and nothing a sinner is, has, or does is acceptable to God in its own merit. The sinner becomes worthy only when Christ makes him so by imputing His own righteousness to him.

The believer has responded to the gospel invitation, has come to the wedding feast. Now he must make sure he will pass the King's inspection—a symbol of the pre-Advent judgment—by wearing the only garment in the universe available to fallen beings that will cover their sinfulness. That is, he must wear the spiritual garment of the saving righteousness of Christ. Only as he satisfies this requirement will the believer have the right to participate in the gospel feast.

2. What Jesus Is Doing to Secure the Believer's Acceptance With the Father

Jesus stands in the holy of holies, now to appear in the presence of God for us. There He ceases not to present His people moment by moment, complete in Himself. . . . We are complete in Him, accepted in the Beloved, only as we abide in Him by faith *(Faith and Works,* p. 107). The provision made is complete, and the eternal righteousness of Christ is placed to the account of every believing soul. The costly, spotless robe, woven in the loom of heaven, has been provided for the repenting, believing sinner. . . . In ourselves we are sinners; but in

19

Christ we are righteous. Having made us righteous through the imputed righteousness of Christ, God pronounces us just, and treats us as just. He looks upon us as His dear children *(Selected Messages,* book 1, p. 394).

Only the covering which Christ Himself has provided can make us meet to appear in God's presence. This covering, the robe of His own righteousness, Christ will put upon every repenting, believing soul *(Christ's Object Lessons,* p. 311). Christ was treated as we deserve, that we might be treated as He deserves. He was condemned for our sins, in which He had no share, that we might be justified by His righteousness, in which we had no share. He suffered the death which was ours, that we might receive the life which was His *(The Desire of Ages,* p. 25).

By His spotless life, His obedience, His death on the cross of Calvary, Christ interceded for the lost race. And now, not as a mere petitioner does the Captain of our salvation intercede for us, but as a Conqueror claiming His victory. His offering is complete, and as our Intercessor He executes His self-appointed work, holding before God the censer containing His own spotless merits and the prayers, confessions, and thanksgiving of His people. Perfumed with the fragrance of His righteousness, these ascend to God as a sweet savor. The offering is wholly acceptable, and pardon covers all transgression *(Christ's Object Lessons,* p. 156).

I will be your representative in heaven. The Father beholds not your faulty character, but He sees you as clothed in My perfection *(The Desire of Ages,* p. 357). Christ will clothe His faithful ones with His own righteousness, that He may present them to His Father "a glorious church, not having spot, or wrinkle, or any such thing" (Eph. 5:27) *(The Great Controversy,* p. 484).

These statements indicate quite persuasively that Christ's mediation in man's behalf is as essential as His death on the cross, because through His mediation He applies the benefits of His redemptive activity to all who respond to the gospel in repentance and faith. Not as a mere petitioner, but as a conqueror claiming His victory, does the Captain of our salvation credit His atoning death, His redemptive victory, and His perfect righteousness to us and thus presents us totally acceptable to the Father.

Notice the following concepts contained in the preceding quotations:

1. As our representative and substitute, Christ presents His people *moment by moment complete in Himself*. So we partake of two different realities at the same time: *in ourselves, by nature, we are sinful; yet in Christ, by faith, we are righteous*. If God were to judge and reward us on the basis of what we are, what we have, and what we do, He would have to let us perish in our fallen condition. However, because God evaluates us on the basis of our faith participation in Christ's merits, He pronounces us just and treats us as His dear children, in spite of the fact that in ourselves we still are sinful, imperfect, and unworthy.

2. Only the covering that Christ Himself has provided can qualify us to appear in God's presence. This garment, a robe woven in the loom of heaven, Christ places upon every repentant, believing individual. And the believer's standing with God—his right to participate in the gospel feast—rests, not on the basis of his own faulty character, but on the fact that he wears Christ's perfection.

3. A transaction takes place between the believer and Christ. The Saviour assumes man's sin, suffers his condemnation, and dies his death. In turn the believer

receives access to Christ's righteousness, is fully justified before God, and participates in the life that rightly belongs to Christ alone.

4. The last passage quoted above does not say that Jesus provides the power the church needs in order to make herself presentable. Instead, it says that He will clothe her so that He may present her a glorious and flawless body. Clothing is never an integral part of those wearing it. It is something that is put upon someone, an outward cover intended to make a person look appropriate. So the passage does not describe the actual reality of the church's true spiritual condition—it does not speak of a real accomplishment of the church. Instead, *the passage describes what Jesus does for the church in order to present her to the Father.* Jesus clothes His people with the robe He Himself provides—the spiritual robe of His own personal righteousness—and thus brings them to the Father as a glorious and flawless church.

Note that Ellen White establishes a direct and necessary relationship between what Christ did for us yesterday as our substitute on the cross and what He is doing for us today as our representative on the throne. Thus, while He completed His redemptive work on our behalf when He gave His life as an atoning sacrifice on the cross, its application to individual believers is a present, ongoing reality that will continue until human probation ceases.

By His atoning sacrifice on the cross the Saviour earned the right to share His personal victory, His personal righteousness, and His personal inheritance with those who become the adopted sons and daughters of God through faith in Him. As our mediator, He now exercises that right by effectually applying to individual believers what He accomplished in principle for all mankind through His vicarious death.

3. The Believer's Sanctification and His Dependence on Christ's Mediation for a Right Standing With God

Ellen White's writings express the idea that sanctification is a lifelong process that, because of its very nature, is never fully completed in the present life. The believer never outgrows his personal sinfulness nor transcends his lost condition. He also never reaches a state of perfect spiritual wholeness nor measures up to the standard of flawless perfection that God requires in a sinless universe. As a result, he remains in a state of constant dependence on Christ's mediation for a right standing with God for as long as he lives.

Sanctification is not the work of a moment, an hour, a day, but of a lifetime. It is not gained by a happy flight of feeling, but is the result of constantly dying to sin, and constantly living for Christ. . . . So long as Satan reigns, we shall have self to subdue, besetting sins to overcome; so long as life shall last, there will be no stopping place, no point which we can reach and say, I have fully attained (*The Acts of the Apostles,* pp. 560, 561). There are hereditary and cultivated tendencies to evil that must be overcome. Appetite and passion must be brought under the control of the Holy Spirit. There is no end to the warfare this side of eternity (*Counsels to Parents and Teachers,* p. 20).

Man may grow up into Christ, his living head. It is not the work of a moment, but that of a lifetime. By growing daily in the divine life, he will not attain to the full stature of a perfect man in Christ until his probation ceases. The growing is a continuous work (*Testimonies,* vol. 4, p. 367).

There are those who have known the pardoning love of Christ and who really desire to be children of God, yet they realize that their character is imperfect, their life faulty, and they are ready to doubt whether their hearts have been renewed by the Holy Spirit. To such I would say, Do not draw back in despair. We shall often have to bow down and weep at the feet of Jesus because of our shortcomings and mistakes, but we are not to be discouraged. Even if we are overcome by the enemy, we are not cast off, not forsaken and rejected of God. No; Christ is at the right hand of God, who also maketh intercession for us. . . . And if you will but yield yourself to Him, He that hath begun a good work in you will carry it forward to the day of Jesus Christ. Pray more fervently; believe more fully *(Steps to Christ,* p. 64).

Such statements lead to at least three significant insights:

1. *Sanctification as a process of change, growth, and maturation, is a genuine reality in the believer's experience.* As he advances in his Christian walk, the disciple of Christ does indeed overcome sinful tendencies, attitudes, and dispositions. He modifies character traits and life habits not consistent with his high calling as a child of God in Christ. Increasingly he reflects the righteous virtues of Christ's holy character in his personal life. And he progressively patterns his life after all that is true and right and loving.

2. Although the believer really grows, develops, and matures as a Christian, *he never reaches the stature of a perfect man or fully attains a state of complete sanctification* during his present life. His battle with both sin and self goes on for as long as he lives. *"There is no end to the warfare this side of eternity."*

3. Only at "the day of Jesus Christ"—at that point in time when the eternal replaces the historical, when the kingdom of glory supersedes the kingdom of grace, and the believer experiences the transformation of nature that takes place at the resurrection/glorification event— will the work that began at conversion reach its total and permanent "completion" (Phil. 1:6).

CHRIST MEDIATES FOR THE BELIEVER

Scripture promises that those who "are children of God" now, during their present existence, will be like Jesus "when he appears," not before (1 John 3:2). When we "see him as he is" (verse 2), "we will be changed. For the perishable must clothe itself with the imperishable, and the mortal with immortality" (1 Cor. 15:52, 53). When God totally and permanently removes all the effects of sin from the redeemed and restores them to the original spiritual wholeness Adam and Eve enjoyed before the Fall, then will the process of their sanctification be complete. That is when all of them "together" will "be made perfect" (Heb. 11:40). As a result of His re-creative/restorative act, the redeemed will for the first time ever be by nature what they now can be only in Christ, by faith.

The battle with sin is only one aspect of sanctification not yet completed in this life. An unending growth, development, and maturation must also go on for as long as life shall last.

> Every believing soul is to conform his will entirely to God's will and keep in a state of repentance and contrition, exercising faith in the atoning merits of the Redeemer and advancing from strength to strength, from glory to glory (*Faith and Works,* p. 103). Sanctification is the work of a lifetime. As our opportunities multiply, our experience will enlarge, and our knowledge increase. We shall become strong to bear responsibility, and our maturity will be in proportion to our privileges (*Christ's Object Lessons,* pp. 65, 66).

> We need constantly a fresh revelation of Christ, a daily experience that harmonizes with His teachings. High and holy attainments are within our reach. Continual progress in knowledge and virtue is God's purpose for us. His law is the echo of His own voice, giving to all the invitation, "Come up higher. Be holy, holier still." Every

day we may advance in perfection of Christian character *(The Ministry of Healing,* p. 503). There should be continual striving and constant progress onward and upward toward perfection of character *(Counsels to Parents and Teachers,* p. 365).

At every advance step in Christian experience our repentance will deepen. It is to those whom the Lord has forgiven, to those whom He acknowledges as His people, that He says, "Then shall ye remember your own evil ways, and your doings that were not good, and shall loathe yourselves in your own sight" (Eze. 36:31). . . . Then our lips will not be opened in self-glorification. We shall know that our sufficiency is in Christ alone. We shall make the apostle's confession our own. "I know that in me (that is, in my flesh) dwelleth no good thing" (Rom. 7:18) *(Christ's Object Lessons,* pp. 160, 161).

These passages clearly indicate that, besides never quite transcending the state of personal sinfulness in which he finds himself, the believer never finishes acquiring the positive virtues of a mature Christian character in this life. His growth is both real and significant, but it is never complete. He always falls short of the glory of God and therefore must live in a state of continual repentance and faith, fully aware that his sufficiency is in Christ alone.

Those who are really seeking to perfect Christian character will never indulge the thought that they are sinless. Their lives may be irreproachable, they may be living representatives of the truth which they have accepted; but the more they discipline their minds to dwell upon the character of Christ, and the nearer they approach to His divine image, the more clearly will they discern *its spotless perfection,* and the more deeply will they feel *their own defects (The Sanctified Life,* p. 7; italics supplied).

Perfection through our own good works we can never attain. The soul who sees Jesus by faith, repudiates his own righteousness. He sees himself as incomplete, his repentance insufficient, his strongest faith but feebleness, his most costly sacrifice as meager, and he sinks in humility at the foot of the cross. But a voice speaks to him from the oracles of God's Word. In amazement he hears the message, "Ye are complete in him" (Col. 2:10). Now all is at rest in his soul. No longer must he strive to find some worthiness in himself, some meritorious deed by which to gain the favor of God *(Faith and Works,* pp. 107, 108).

The individual who sees Jesus by faith does not downgrade himself because he is still a sinner. His problem is not that he is entirely without either positive qualities or good works, but that they are all imperfect. He admittedly has a degree of righteousness, repentance, faith, sacrifice. But *because he has had a view of the perfection of Christ, he has both the point of reference and the spiritual perception needed to realize that he falls short of God's standard of perfect righteousness, and therefore deserves, not God's approval, but His condemnation.* His perception of Christ enables him to see the imperfection of what he is, the inadequacy of what he has, and the insufficiency of what he does. It leads him to realize his total dependence on Christ, and moves him to sink in humility at the foot of the cross.

But then, when he perceives his real predicament as a lost sinner, realizes his total dependence on Christ for any standing with God, and in humility bows down at the foot of the cross, he hears the good news of the gospel—all the good news the gospel can give him today, during his present historical life. That is, the news that all is well: he is complete in Christ, accepted in the Beloved, and therefore does not have to "strive to find some worthiness in himself, some meritorious deed

27

by which to gain the favor of God."

At the second coming of Jesus, when God restores the believer to the original perfection with which He created man in the beginning, he will be righteous by nature, just as our first parents were before the Fall. In the meantime he can be righteous, holy, worthy, a son of God, only in Christ. He totally depends on Christ's mediation for acceptance with the Father, and consequently must live by faith in Him to the very end of his life.

It is therefore logical—even imperative—to conclude that the first reason Ellen White's writings consider the mediatorial ministry of Christ essential to the plan of salvation is that this ministry constitutes the only way for a sinner to secure a right standing with God. Jesus mediates for the believer to present him—as an individual person—perfectly righteous before the Father. *The Saviour imputes His atoning death, His redemptive victory, and His saving righteousness to the believer so that he may by faith stand before God faultless in Christ in spite of the fact that by nature he is still sinful, imperfect, and unworthy in himself.*

4. Some Scriptural Considerations

As I indicated in the introduction, this book is not a doctrinal statement based on an exhaustive investigation of Scripture, but a study attempting to systematize and articulate Ellen White's writings on the mediation of Christ. Therefore I bring in the scriptural evidence only to show that her concepts are consistent with the Bible and therefore reliable. That is, they have doctrinal value because they harmonize with Scripture.

The first passage we will examine is Hebrews 7:25: "Therefore he is able to save completely those who come to God through him, because he always lives to intercede for them." This verse contains at least three significant concepts:

1. Jesus is "able to save" by living "to intercede" for us. Thus text establishes a direct cause-effect relationship between Christ's mediation and our salvation. As the living mediator, Jesus does something now that is essential to salvation—today He makes salvation a reality for us. This justifies the Ellen White passage that states that the mediation of Christ is as vital to the plan of salvation as was His death on the cross (*The Great Controversy,* p. 489).

2. By mediating on their behalf, Jesus saves "those who come to God through him." Clearly He does not save everyone, but only a specific group. His mediation does not include those who want to find a different way to the Father, who attempt to achieve a proper standing with Him on the basis of their own achievements—their personal righteousness and "perfect" obedience.

"Access . . . into this grace" (Rom. 5:2) is possible only through faith in Jesus and granted only to those who seek to be right with God on the basis of His redemptive work. But when someone wants to achieve the same objective through his personal spiritual accomplishments, he creates a different way of salvation and consequently loses what is available to those who come by Christ. That is what Paul teaches when he states, "You are severed from Christ, you who would be justified by the law; you have fallen away from grace" (Gal. 5:4, RSV).

In other words, the resources available to those who participate in God's covenant of grace are not accessible to those who endeavor to find another way to approach God. If they do not center their assurance of salvation on Christ's redemptive work, then they stand completely on their own. (They have rejected God's provision. He cannot cancel their condemnation or give them Christ's merits to make up for their spiritual destitution.) Ellen White expresses the same principle when she says that "in ourselves we are sinners; but in Christ we are righteous" (*Selected Messages,* book 1, p. 394), that *"we are complete in Him, accepted in the Beloved, only as we abide in Him by faith"* (*Faith and Works,* p. 107; italics supplied).

3. Jesus "is able to save completely"—"to the uttermost" (KJV), "fully and completely" (Phillips), "absolutely" (NEB), "for all time" (RSV)—"those who come to God through him." As "the author and perfecter of our faith" (Heb. 12:2), He saves not partially, but completely.

The following passage speaks of those who want to win salvation by good works:

> Jesus, they think, will do some of the saving; they must do the rest. They need to see by faith the righteousness of Christ as their only hope for time and for eternity (*Faith and Works,* p. 26).

Paul says that Jesus will "present you holy and blameless and irreproachable before him, provided that you continue in the faith, stable and steadfast, not shifting from the hope of the gospel" (Col. 1:22, 23, RSV). Notice that the text does not state that Jesus will enable the believers to develop perfect righteousness or attain spiritual wholeness, but that He will *present them* as being holy, blameless, and irreproachable before God. As in Hebrews 7:25, Jude 24, Ephesians 5:27, etc., this is a reference, not to something the believers actually achieve in their personal historical lives, but to what Christ does for them.

The second scriptural passage we want to study briefly is Matthew 22:1-14. It records Christ's parable of the wedding feast, or the parable of the man without a wedding garment, which provides much of the symbolism used in Ellen White's writings. And since we are examining several scriptural passages to find the sources of some of her concepts, we will discuss the parable together with the following statement:

> When the king came in to view the guests, the real character of all was revealed. For every guest at the feast there had been provided a wedding garment. This garment was a gift from the king. By wearing it the guests showed their respect for the giver of the feast. But one man was clothed in his common citizen dress. He had refused to make the preparation required by the king. The garment provided for him at great cost he disdained to wear. Thus he insulted his lord (*Christ's Object Lessons*, p. 309).

At least six points catch our attention here:

1. The king urged the servants in charge of bringing the guests to the wedding feast to "go to the street corners and invite to the banquet anyone you find. So the servants . . . gathered all the people they could find, both good and bad, and the wedding hall was filled with guests" (verses 9, 10). Anyone, whether good or bad, who accepted the invitation could enter the wedding hall.

2. The king's inspection of the guests—an act of judgment—determined who would and who would not be received as guests and allowed to actually participate in the wedding feast. The criterion used did not center on the moral character of those who came—whether they were good or bad. Instead, it involved their relationship to the wedding garment he personally provided for them—whether they wore it or not. So the outcome of this inspection disclosed, not the goodness and worthiness of the guests, but the generosity of the

king. Anyone who dressed in the king's garment could be a guest and join in the wedding feast. On the other hand, anyone who, by the very act, failed to put on the king's garment disqualified himself as a guest.

3. Through this unique requirement of wearing the wedding garment, the king placed everyone on the same level. No one could attribute his acceptance either to his superior moral goodness or to the higher quality of the garment he personally chose to wear before coming to the banquet. Whether a particular guest was a little better than his neighbors, or was dressed in more expensive clothes than what others could afford, played no role here. They were all equally dependent on something the king provided as a gift—a unique garment that they could neither secure anywhere else nor produce themselves by any means whatsoever. Because the garment was the king's free gift, they all had the same opportunity to possess it, and no one had a valid excuse for not wearing it.

4. As it turned out, only one man refused the preparation required by the king. The king did not cast him out of the hall because he was the worst among the "bad" people that had come. As far as the parable is concerned, he could have been the best among the "good." Nor did he get rejected because his own garment was ugly, defective, or unclean. The would-be guest had to go into darkness because he wore the wrong garment. Instead of being clothed in what the king had provided, he wore something he had either produced himself or acquired by his own means somewhere else.

5. By wearing his own clothing instead of the king's wedding garment, he insulted his lord. As a result, he not only got excluded from the wedding—as did those who refused the invitation and did not come—but also

was punished for refusing to comply with the specific conditions established by the king. He either ignored or attempted to violate the king's order, an order according to which "only those are received who have put on the robe of Christ's righteousness" *(ibid.,* p. 312).

6. Verse 14 states that "many are invited, but few are chosen." Actually God calls everyone, since Christ's redemptive work embraces all mankind—the gospel leaves out absolutely no one. Who, then, are the few "chosen"? According to the parable, the chosen were those who did three basic things: (1) they all accepted the king's invitation to the wedding feast, (2) they all came to the wedding hall, and (3) they all dressed themselves in the wedding garment. By putting on the garment, and thus making the preparation required by the king, they demonstrated, first, that they were the truly obedient, and second, that they had genuine faith. They based their assurance of acceptance with the king, not on who they were, what they had, or what they did on their own, but on the wedding garment, which symbolizes the saving righteousness of Christ freely imparted to every one who repents and believes.

The third and last passage we want to discuss is Galatians 3:26-4:7. Two concepts particularly interest us at this point. First: "You are all sons of God through faith in Christ Jesus" (Gal. 3:26). Adoption, by definition the granting of sonship to someone who is not a natural son, is one of the first benefits believers receive through faith in Jesus Christ. The Saviour bestows "the right to become children of God"—"to all who received him, to those who believed in his name" (John 1:12). The believers are thus "adopted as [God's] sons through Jesus Christ" (Eph. 1:5). Sonship, then, is not something believers earn, but a gift of God's grace to those who accept Jesus Christ as their personal Saviour.

Second: "If you belong to Christ, then you are . . . heirs according to the promise" (Gal. 3:29). "So you are no longer a slave, but a son; and since you are a son, God has made you also an heir" (Gal. 4:7). We observe a clear cause-effect relationship here, a chain reaction, if you please. 1. The believer becomes an adopted son of God on the basis of his faith relationship to Jesus Christ—his faith in Jesus entitles him to sonship. 2. And he becomes an heir because he is an adopted child of God—his sonship entitles him to the inheritance. In other words, sonship belongs to those who have faith in Jesus Christ, and the inheritance—eternal life with all that it entails—belongs to those who are sons of God in Christ.

This direct cause-effect relationship between faith and sonship, on the one hand, and sonship and heirship, on the other, must remain intact. The Scriptures teach that the children of God grow in all aspects of their lives. But the Bible never establishes a cause-effect relationship between the degree of a Christian's spiritual development and his right to the eternal inheritance. Human parents divide their estate among all their children irrespective of their relative ages, sizes, and degrees of maturity. Even our imperfect sense of justice tells us it would be extremely unfair to disinherit a child because he was still a youngster and consequently had not yet reached full maturity.

As a result of his long life with God, Methuselah experienced a relatively high degree of maturation. But that by no means renders him better qualified to receive the eternal inheritance than the thief on the cross who, because of his adoption at the eleventh hour, died as a babe in Christ. Both cases illustrate the fact that the eternal inheritance belongs to the sons and daughters of God in Christ regardless of their degree of spiritual growth. The babes in Christ who must face the final judgment—either at death or at the end of probation—shortly after their birth into God's spiritual family have exactly the same right, granted by grace, to be heirs as do those who are old and seasoned "adults."

The mature child of God, who has experienced a real and significant amount of spiritual growth, never becomes anything other than what he was initially. He always remains an adopted son whose right to the inheritance rests on the fact that he is a child of God in Christ, and not on the degree of growth he experiences during his life as a Christian. Whether he dies as a newly born babe in Christ or lives a long life of growth and development makes no difference as far as his right to the inheritance is concerned. He is an heir strictly because he is a son, and a son only because of adoption.

This explains from a different angle the same concept we saw earlier: namely, that although we will never attain a state of total sanctification in this life, we can have full assurance of salvation. Although we are sinful in ourselves by nature, we are righteous in Christ by faith. Because of the imputation of Christ's righteousness to us, God declares us righteous and treats us as His children in spite of the fact that we are still sinful, imperfect, and unworthy. So God does not judge and reward us on the basis of our relative progress in character development and behavior modification, but rather on our acceptance of the Saviour's redemptive work.

II Christ Mediates for the Believer to Make His Performance—His Obedience, Service, Worship—Acceptable to the Father.

Many Ellen White statements speak of another aspect, a second dimension, of Christ's mediatorial ministry. They indicate that besides presenting the believers, as individual persons, moment by moment complete in Himself, Jesus makes their performance—their life as adopted children of God in Christ—perfectly acceptable to the Father.

As far as I know, no one has ever published a study on this aspect of Christ's mediatorial ministry. Apparently the students of Ellen White's writings have either overlooked it or failed to see its significance. We will therefore attempt to substantiate it here. First, we see *why* the believer needs Christ to mediate for his performance. Then we investigate *how*, according to Ellen White, the mediatorial ministry of Christ perfects the believer's actions so that they may meet the standard God requires.

1. Why the Believer Depends on Christ's Mediation in Order to Render Perfect Obedience.

The Christian's need to depend on Christ's mediation in order to render acceptable performance rests, first, on the absolute nature of the standard of perfection God has established, and second, on his own limitations as a sinner to meet the demands of the law.

HIS OBEDIENCE, SERVICE, WORSHIP

God requires at this time just what He required of the holy pair in Eden—perfect obedience to His requirements. His law remains the same in all ages. The great standard of righteousness presented in the Old Testament is not lowered in the New *(Faith and Works,* p. 52). The condition of eternal life is now just what it always has been—just what it was in Paradise before the fall of our first parents—perfect obedience to the law of God, perfect righteousness *(Steps to Christ,* p. 62).

Many are deceived as to their true condition before God. They congratulate themselves upon the wrong acts which they do not commit, and forget to enumerate the good and noble deeds which God requires of them, but which they have neglected to perform *(The Great Controversy,* p. 601). The law demands perfect obedience. . . . The least deviation from its requirements, by neglect or willful transgression, is sin, and every sin exposes the sinner to the wrath of God *(Selected Messages,* book 1, p. 218). Higher than the highest human thought can reach is God's ideal for His children. Godliness—godlikeness—is the goal to be reached *(Education,* p. 18).

We call attention to only three aspects of her statements: 1. The standard we must reach is not just obedience but *flawless obedience,* total compliance with God's will for humanity—mere approximations to perfection are not acceptable. 2. *The least deviation* from God's requirements is sin, and *every sin* exposes a person to the wrath of God. 3. Men are guilty not only for *doing evil* deeds but also for *not doing enough good* deeds.

Perfect obedience means the satisfaction of both the letter and the spirit of God's revealed word. It demands absolute harmony with all the divine principles that underlie *His entire will for man.* Anything short of this is imperfect obedience—an obedience that, instead of receiving God's approval, deserves His condemnation.

37

As a result, someone may never have violated a single specific prohibition of the Decalogue—such as taking God's name in vain, coveting, or bearing false witness—and still be condemned because he failed either to make God first or to love all his neighbors as himself all the time and under all circumstances. He neglected *"justice* and *mercy* and *faith,"* which, according to Jesus, are *"the weightier matters of the law"* (Matt. 23:23, RSV).

The question as to whether the believer can meet God's standard of perfect obedience Ellen White answered both negatively and positively in her writings:

No. Because he is a sinner, the believer cannot render perfect obedience to God, unless . . .

It was possible for Adam, before the fall, to form a righteous character by obedience to God's law. But he failed to do this, and because of his sin our natures are fallen and we cannot make ourselves righteous. Since we are sinful, unholy, we cannot perfectly obey the holy law. We have no righteousness of our own with which to meet the claims of the law of God. But Christ has made a way of escape for us *(Steps to Christ,* p. 62).

Righteousness is obedience to the law. The law demands righteousness, and this the sinner owes to the law; but he is incapable of rendering it *(Selected Messages,* book 1, p. 367). It [the law] could not justify man, because in his sinful nature he could not keep the law *(Patriarchs and Prophets,* p. 373). God will not bring His law down to meet the imperfect standard of man; and man cannot meet the demands of that holy law without exercising repentance toward God and faith toward our Lord Jesus Christ *(Faith and Works,* p. 29).

Yes. In spite of his sinfulness, the believer can render perfect obedience to God, provided . . .

By His perfect obedience He has made it possible for every human being to obey God's commandments. . . . Christ came in the form of humanity, and by His perfect obedience He proved that humanity and divinity combined can obey every one of God's precepts (*Christ's Object Lessons,* pp. 312-314).

The cross of Christ testifies to the immutability of the law of God. . . . Jesus died that He might ascribe unto the repenting sinner His own righteousness, and make it possible for man to keep the law (*Selected Messages,* book 1, p. 312).

An obvious tension exists between the two statements we have quoted. If taken at face value, they appear to contradict each other. However, when we examine them more carefully and study them on a broader basis, we find out that they do not contradict but complement each other. They belong to a type of writings that we should not consider to be either comprehensive, systematic, or conclusive. Instead, we must see them as partial statements that she never meant to constitute the full answer to the question they address. They merely point to a truth that is both deeper and broader than what they specifically express—a truth that, once understood, discloses their complementary nature and essential harmony.

The first set of statements actually affirms that, because he is a sinner, the believer cannot render perfect obedience to God *without partaking* of what Christ makes available through His mediatorial ministry. In turn the second set states that, in spite of his personal sinfulness, the believer can meet God's standard of perfect obedience, *provided that he participates in* what Christ makes available to him.

Notice again: "Man cannot meet the demands of that holy law *without* exercising repentance toward God and faith toward our Lord Jesus Christ." Through repentance the believer secures God's forgiveness and through faith he becomes a participant in Christ's saving righteousness—both of which are made available to him through the mediation of Christ. So the problem is not that the law is unreasonably demanding, but that fallen man is incapable of obeying it perfectly. In turn the solution is not to attempt to transcend our sinfulness—for that is not possible in this life—but to become participants in the victory and merits of Christ.

2. How the Mediator Makes the Believer's Performance Perfectly Acceptable to God.

We have seen that, according to Ellen White, God requires not just obedience, but perfect obedience. And we have suggested that she also indicates that such obedience is possible only through the believer's repentance toward God and his faith in Jesus. Now we shall endeavor to establish exactly *how* the mediation of Christ makes it possible for the believer to meet the standard God has established.

> Christ, *in the victories achieved in His death* on Calvary's cross, plainly lays open the way for man, and thus makes it possible for him to keep the law of God through the Way, the Truth, and the Life. There is no other way *(Selected Messages,* book 1, p. 342). Jesus became the Mediator between God and man, to restore the repenting soul to favor with God by giving him grace to keep the law of the Most High *(Faith and Works,* p. 119, italics supplied). Through the grace of Christ we shall live in obedience to the law of God written upon our hearts *(Patriarchs and Prophets,* p. 372). No sin can be tolerated in those who shall walk with Christ in white. The filthy garments are to be removed, and Christ's robe of righteousness is to be placed upon us. By repentance and faith we are enabled to render obedience to all the commandments of God,

and are found without blame before Him (*Testimonies,* vol. 5, p. 472). Only through faith in Christ is [perfect] obedience [to the requirements of the law] possible (*In Heavenly Places,* p. 146).

Through faith in Christ obedience to every principle of the law is made possible (*The SDA Bible Commentary,* Ellen G. White Comments, vol. 6, p. 1077). In order to meet the requirements of the law, our faith must grasp the righteousness of Christ, accepting it as our righteousness. Through union with Christ, *through acceptance of His righteousness by faith,* we may be qualified to work the works of God, to be colaborers with Christ (*Selected Messages,* book 1, p. 374, italics supplied). Christ became the sinless sacrifice for a guilty race, making men prisoners of hope, so that through repentance toward God because they had broken His holy law, and through faith in Christ as their Substitute, Surety, and righteousness, they might be brought back to loyalty to God and to obedience to His holy law (*Faith and Works,* p. 118).

We will examine three ideas appearing in her statements: 1. Perfect obedience to God's will is possible to the believer. 2. The only way to achieve it is through Jesus Christ—"through the Way, the Truth, and the Life. There is no other way." 3. God's grace, the righteousness of Christ, and the believer's repentance and faith are the true key to perfect obedience.

Our examination of Ellen White's writings has led us to a somewhat surprising discovery: They consistently teach that *perfect obedience* to God's will is possible *only* when, through faith, the believer participates in what Christ does for him as his mediator and substitute in the Father's presence.

Christ's mediation makes the believer's obedience perfectly acceptable to the Father in three distinct yet interrelated ways: (1) through substitution, (2) through purification, and (3) through complementarity. What follows, grouped under these three headings, is but a sample of her statements.

a. Perfect obedience through *substitution.* The Father accepts the all-sufficient righteousness of Christ— His holy character, His perfect merits, and His flawless obedience—*in place of* the believer's imperfections, shortcomings, and sinfulness.

Since we are sinful, unholy, we cannot perfectly obey the holy law. We have no righteousness of our own with which to meet the claims of the law of God. But Christ has made a way of escape for us. He lived on earth amid trials and temptations such as we have to meet. He lived a sinless life. He died for us, and now He offers to take our sins and give us His righteousness. If you give yourself to Him, and accept Him as your Saviour, then, sinful as your life may have been, for His sake you are accounted righteous. Christ's character stands in place of your character, and you are accepted before God just as if you had not sinned *(Steps to Christ,* p. 62).

The only way in which he [the sinner] can attain to righteousness is through faith. By faith he can bring to God the merits of Christ, and the Lord places the obedience of His Son to the sinner's account. Christ's righteousness is accepted in place of man's failure, and God receives, pardons, justifies, the repentant, believing soul, treats him as though he were righteous, and loves him as He loves His Son. This is how faith is accounted righteousness; and the pardoned soul goes on from grace to grace, from light to a greater light *(Selected Messages,* book 1, p. 367).

The moment the sinner believes in Christ, he stands in the sight of God uncondemned; for the righteousness of Christ is his: Christ's perfect obedience is imputed to him *(Fundamentals of Christian Education,* p. 429). The truth is plain, and when it is contrasted with error, its character may be discerned. All the subjects of God's grace may understand what is required of them. By faith we may conform our lives to the standard of righteousness, because we can appropriate to ourselves the righteousness of Christ *(Faith and Works,* p. 97).

b. Perfect obedience through *purification.* Like a purifying incense, the saving righteousness of Christ *cleanses* the believer's worship, obedience, and service of their sinfulness makes them acceptable to God.

Before the believer is held out the wonderful possibility of being like Christ, obedient to all the principles of the law. But of himself man is utterly unable to reach this condition. The holiness that God's Word declares he must have before he can be saved is the result of the working of divine grace as he bows in submission to the discipline and restraining influences of the Spirit of truth. Man's obedience can be made perfect only by the incense of Christ's righteousness, which fills with divine fragrance every act of obedience *(The Acts of the Apostles,* p. 532).

The incense, ascending with the prayers of Israel, represents the merits and intercession of Christ, His perfect righteousness, which through faith is imputed to His people, and which can alone make the worship of sinful beings acceptable to God *(Patriarchs and Prophets,* p. 353). Neither time nor events can lessen the efficacy of the atoning sacrifice. As the fragrant cloud of incense rose acceptably to heaven, and Aaron sprinkled the blood upon the mercy seat of ancient Israel and cleansed the people from guilt, so the merits of the slain Lamb are accepted by God today as a purifier from the defilement of sin *(Testimonies,* vol. 4, p. 124).

All must be laid upon the fire of Christ's righteousness to cleanse it from its earthly odor before it rises in a cloud of fragrant incense to the great Jehovah and is accepted as

a sweet savor. . . . Christ for our sakes became poor, that
we through His poverty might be made rich. And any
works that man can render to God will be far less than
nothingness. My requests are made acceptable only because they are laid upon Christ's righteousness. The idea
of doing anything to merit the grace of pardon is fallacy
from beginning to end. "Lord, in my hand no price I
bring, simply to Thy cross I cling" *(Faith and Works,* p. 24).

Christ looks at the spirit, and when He sees us
carrying our burden with faith, His perfect holiness
atones for our shortcomings. When we do our best, He
becomes our righteousness *(Selected Messages,* book 1, p.
368). The merit of Jesus must be mingled with our
prayers and efforts, or they are as worthless as was the
offering of Cain. Could we see all the activity of human
instrumentality, as it appears before God, we would see
that only the work accomplished by much prayer, which is
sanctified by the merit of Christ, will stand the test of the
judgment *(Christian Service,* p. 263).

c. Perfect obedience through *complementation.*
Christ takes the believer's honest, though imperfect,
efforts to live in harmony with God's will and *completes*
them—He perfects them—with His own merits so that
they meet the divine requirements.

Faith and works go hand in hand; they act harmoni-
ously in the work of overcoming. Works without faith are
dead, and faith without works is dead. Works will never
save us; it is the merit of Christ that will avail in our
behalf. Through faith in Him, Christ will make all our
imperfect efforts acceptable to God *(Faith and Works,* p.
48). Although the good works of man are of no more
value without faith in Jesus than was the offering of Cain,
yet covered with the merit of Christ, they testify [to] the
worthiness of the doer to inherit eternal life *(Selected
Messages,* book 1, p. 382).

The life of Christ is a perfect fulfillment of every precept of [the] law. He says, "I have kept my father's commandments." The knowledge of the law would condemn the sinner, and crush hope from his breast, if he did not see Jesus as his substitute and surety, ready to pardon his transgression, and to forgive his sin. When, through faith in Jesus Christ, man does according to the very best of his ability, and seeks to keep the way of the Lord by obedience to the Ten Commandments, the perfection of Christ is imputed to cover the transgression of the repentant and obedient soul *(Fundamentals of Christian Education,* p. 135).

Through the merits of the Redeemer, *God accepts the efforts of sinful man* in keeping His law, which is holy, just, and good *(Sons and Daughters of God,* p. 41; italics supplied). When it is in the heart to obey God, when efforts are put forth to this end, Jesus accepts this disposition and effort as man's best service, and *He makes up for the deficiency with His own divine merit (My Life Today,* p. 250; italics supplied).

Although the following passage refers specifically to prayer, it helps us to understand how, according to Ellen White, the mediation of Christ perfects the believer's deficient performance.

Every sincere prayer is heard in heaven. It may not be fluently expressed; but if the heart is in it, it will ascend to the sanctuary where Jesus ministers, and He will present it to the Father without one awkward, stammering word, beautiful and fragrant with the incense of His own perfection *(The Desire of Ages,* p. 667).

Clearly Christ's mediation has a double effect upon the "sincere prayer": 1. It removes the imperfections the prayer had as expressed by the petitioner. 2. It makes it "beautiful" with the incense of Christ's own perfection.

These considerations lead us to conclude that, according to Ellen White, Christ's mediatorial ministry is as essential as His death on the cross because through it He brings the plan of salvation to effectual realization for those who accept Him as their personal Saviour, by sharing with them the benefits of the redemptive work He completed at the cross. This sharing happens in a double way: 1. Christ imputes His atoning death, His redemptive victory, and His saving righteousness to the believer and thus presents him—as an individual person—perfectly righteous before the Father. 2. Christ imputes His personal merits to the believer's deficient life as a son of God and thus makes his obedience, his service, and his worship pleasing to the Father.

3. Some Scriptural Considerations.

While some details contained in the statements previously discussed do not appear in the Bible, the basic concepts they present are thoroughly scriptural. The passages we discuss in this section should show the correlation. Paul states:

> Just as the result of one trespass was condemnation for all men, so also the result of one act of righteousness was justification that brings life for all men. For just as through the disobedience of the one man the many were made sinners, so also through the obedience of the one man the many will be made righteous (Rom. 5:18, 19).

Notice two basic points here: 1. The justification of the sinner rests not on what he is or on what he does—such as a perfect character or a flawless obedience—but on Christ's "act of righteousness." 2. "The many [a direct reference to the redeemed] will be made righteous" "through the obedience of the one man," namely Jesus Christ.

We have seen that, according to Ellen White, "the moment the sinner believes in Christ, he stands in the sight of God uncondemned; for the righteousness of Christ is his: Christ's perfect obedience is imputed to him." The believer "can bring to God the merits of Christ, and the Lord places the obedience of His Son to the sinner's account." Although the passage in Romans does not use these exact words, it is clear that it establishes the same principle. Paul reveals the fact that Christ's act of righteousness results in "justification that brings life for all men." He thus indicates that the obedience of Jesus counts for—or is credited to—the believer so that the believer is made righteous on the basis of Christ's obedience imputed to him by faith.

The fact that Christ's mediation completes and perfects the partial compliance and imperfect efforts of the believer does not do away with the necessity of obedience, however. Jesus does not make conscious transgression and deliberate disobedience acceptable to God—only forgiveness, through repentance and confession can remedy that. Instead, it is the believer's true attempts to live a life worthy of God's adopted children in Christ (Eph. 4:1ff; 5:8ff) that the Saviour's righteousness cleanses of sin and makes perfect in the Father's sight.

Scripture teaches that Jesus "became the source of eternal salvation for all who obey him" (Heb. 5:9). This means that Jesus is the Saviour, not of those who consciously reject and deliberately contradict God's will for their lives, but only of those who obey Him. It also indicates that those who obey Him need Jesus as their Saviour. Not their obedience, but Christ is the source—the cause, the basis—of their salvation.

The "obedient" need a Saviour, not because they do wrong in obeying, but because God never planned obedience to be another method to achieve saving righteousness—it is not the way for fallen beings to transcend their lost condition, outgrow their personal sinfulness, or achieve a state of spiritual wholeness. Paul states that "if a law had been given that could impart life, then righteousness would certainly have come by the law" (Gal. 3:21). That is why no amount of obedience can give us access to salvation. Because eternal life exists only in Christ, we can have access to it only by possessing Him.

The second reason the obedient need a Saviour is that their obedience, being partial and imperfect, instead of earning them God's favor, actually deserves His condemnation. That is why the One who is the "author and perfecter ["finisher," KJV] of our faith, who . . . endured the cross . . . and sat down at the right hand of the throne of God" (Heb. 12:2), must originate redemption and bring it to completion (Phil. 11:6).

Peter states that the believer's spiritual sacrifices— his worship, prayers, obedience, service—are acceptable to God through Jesus Christ (1 Peter 2:5). Evidently the basis on which God accepts the believer's gifts of love and witness, praise and obedience, worship and service, is not the value of the gift or the merits of the giver. Instead, God responds favorably to them only when— and by reason of the fact that—the believer brings them through Jesus Christ, the mediator, who cleanses them of sin, removes their imperfection, and perfects them through the imputation of His personal merits. Only by approaching the Father through Christ does the believer show that he recognizes his true condition.

4. The Obedience of Faith

Since there is no uniform understanding of what constitutes true obedience, we will briefly discuss the subject at this point. Some believe that in obedience it is the motive that counts. If the motive is selfish, then the obedience is worthless. But if the motive is love, then the obedience is genuine and pleasing to God. According to this view, a person's capacity to love holds the key to true obedience.

Others say that the difference between legalistic obedience and the obedience God requires lies in the power that the individual uses. If one obeys in one's own strength, then his response is legalistic and consequently unacceptable. However, if one obeys in the power of the Spirit, then one's obedience is true and genuine. Thus a person's capacity to use the power of the Spirit holds the key to perfect obedience.

Still others argue that we achieve true obedience when we precisely keep all ten commandments of the moral law. In their view, sin is no more than transgression of the letter of the law, narrowly defined as the Decalogue. Therefore if one does what it commands and abstains from what it forbids, then he renders true, total, and flawless obedience—an obedience acceptable on its own merits because it fully satisfies the standard set by God.

Obviously all three views have some merit—they are genuine and necessary parts of the answer. But they do not provide the complete explanation to what constitutes perfect obedience. Let us consider each view:

1. Love is indeed the only true motive. But love does not dictate what is good and what is evil. It cannot determine the moral quality of a deed, nor has it any power to make a wrong into a right. So unless one is properly informed and rightly guided by the principles of the moral order by which God rules the universe, love can prompt him to do something contrary to what is

truly good, right, and loving. Right motives and good intentions do not always lead to actions in harmony with God's will.

2. To say that the kind of power we use determines the nature of our obedience is inadequate for two basic reasons. First, it is inadequate because the injunctions of the law either command or prohibit us to do something without specifying either the method we must follow or the power we must employ in order to obey. For example, the commandment does not say "You shall not steal through the power of the Spirit." Instead, it says "You shall not steal," period. Therefore, if we have indeed refrained from stealing, then we have obeyed all this specific commandment requires of us. How we managed to obey is totally irrelevant as far as the demands of the law are concerned.

Second, and more importantly to make a distinction between obeying through the power of the Spirit and complying in our own strength creates a false antithesis. According to Scripture, the sinful nature of fallen man neither wants nor is able to obey God's will. Notice this passage from Paul:

> The sinful mind is hostile to God. It does not submit to God's law, nor can it do so. Those controlled by the sinful nature cannot please God. You, however, are controlled not by the sinful nature but by the Spirit (Rom 8:7-9).

We therefore conclude that no fallen being ever endeavors to obey God's will all on his own. By himself he has neither the will nor the power to do what is right. His sinful mind does not want to submit to God's will, and his sinful nature does not have the strength such conformity requires. In view of this, we further conclude that, to the extent that a sinful being obeys God at all, to that extent he is also responding to the prompt-ings and acting by the enabling power of the Spirit.

3. The view that true obedience means faithful compliance with all ten commandments of the law falls short because God's will for fallen man transcends the specific commands and prohibitions contained in the Decalogue. As a partial statement of God's will for us, the law tells us only what we must do in order to live morally right, but it has nothing to say concerning what we must do to be saved. The law evaluates our behavior and tells us wherein we have sinned, but it does not explain to us how to be free of our guilt and have our condemnation revoked; nor does it reveal to us all that we must do in order to continue living in a proper relationship with God once we have been accepted into His fellowship. In other words, the law discloses that we are sinners but does not say how we are to be saved from our sin. It reminds us that we need a Saviour but does not say how or where we can find Him.

God's instructions—His decrees, statutes, and com-mands—telling us what to do to remedy our sin problem do not appear in the Decalogue. We find them only in the gospel as expressed in both Testaments of Scripture. Briefly stated, the Old Testament sinner had to bring, for example, a lamb as a sin offering to the tabernacle, confess his sin on its head, and kill it so the priest could use the lamb's blood to make atonement and secure God's forgiveness for him (Lev. 4-6). Failure to obey the laws regulating this ceremony had much greater conse-quences than rendering less than flawless obedience to the Decalogue. *God had made provision for those whose obedience did not measure up to the demands of the law, but none for those who failed to secure His forgiveness through the means He provided.*

51

This is a clear indication that the decision concerning whether a particular Israelite was obedient or not ultimately depended, not on his relationship to the law, but on his relationship to the lamb God provided as a symbol of Christ. We therefore conclude that, according to the Old Testament, the truly obedient were those who, having done their best to live in full harmony with the laws of God, recognized their transgression and shortcoming and came to God with the blood of a sacrifice to secure His forgiveness, and thus retain their place as members of God's covenant people. True obedience obviously included both submission to the injunctions of the moral law and compliance with the demands of the gospel as represented in the tabernacle services.

The same is true in the New Testament. Jesus stated plainly that He had not "come to abolish the Law or the Prophets . . . but to fulfill them" (Mat. 5:17). He did not come to free us of the responsibility to live morally right, or to abolish the principles that govern God's creation so that we may please our sinful nature at will. But saying so does most definitely not mean that every time Jesus urged His listeners to keep either His own or the Father's commands He referred specifically to the Ten Commandments. Nor does it mean that the Saviour's call to discipleship imposes no further obligations than what the law requires—that His demands on us begin and end with what the Decalogue spells out.

When we read Christ's assertion "If you love me, you will obey what I command" (John 14:15), many of us almost automatically think He is referring to the Ten Commandments. We must remember, however, that Jesus is here speaking primarily in His role as Saviour. Therefore the expression "obey what I command," though it may include the Decalogue, it is most certainly not limited to it. Christ's command focuses especially on the demands and obligations that the gospel imposes on the believer. It deals not just with what we must do in order to "live a life worthy of the calling" we received, as Paul puts it (Eph. 4:1), but especially with what we must do in order to respond to this calling so that we may be reconciled to the Father and receive the adoption as sons and daughters of God.

The directives of the gospel originate in its particular nature and contribute to the realization of its unique objectives. Therefore they are essentially different from the injunctions of the law. Needless to say, the demands of the gospel are as binding and normative as those of the law. The salvation God provides in Christ demands certain specific responses from the sinner. For example, when during His earthly ministry Jesus proclaimed the good news of God, saying, "The time is fulfilled, and the kingdom of God is at hand; repent, and believe in the gospel" (Mark 1:15, RSV), He did more than appeal to the conscience of His listeners. He, in fact, made repentance and faith mandatory for any sinner seeking reconciliation with God. In the process, He revealed that they are a test of a sinner's obedience as truly as any of the commandments of the law.

Luke reports that as "the word of God spread," "a large number of priests became obedient to the faith" (Acts 6:7). We can be sure that many of these priests were as faithful to the law as is reasonable to expect of any fallen being. Like Paul they were "faultless" according to the law (Phil. 3:6). However, had they not become obedient to the gospel, they would have had no access to grace and hence no hope of eternal life.

Paul received "apostleship to call people from among all the Gentiles to the obedience that comes from faith" (Rom. 1:5). "The obedience of faith" (RSV) comes only from those who have accepted Jesus Christ as their personal Saviour. *Without this faith-participation in the redemptive work of Christ, no amount of law-keeping will be able to reconcile us to God, grant us the right of adoption, and give us access to the Father's eternal inheritance.*

Jesus revealed that the demands of the gospel are mandatory when He said that "whoever believes in him shall not perish but have eternal life" and "whoever does not believe stands condemned already because he has not believed in the name of God's one and only Son" (John 3:16,18). Clearly a person's eternal destiny depends not on whether he obeys the law—if that were the standard no one would ever be saved—but on whether he responds as demanded by the gospel. Paul expressed the same point when he stated that "those who do not know God and do not obey the gospel of our Lord Jesus" "will be punished with everlasting destruction and shut out from the presence of the Lord" (2 Thess. 1:8, 9). As was the case in Old Testament times, God has made provision for our failure to render flawless obedience to the law, but none for those who do not respond as the gospel demands.

It is therefore logical to conclude that, according to the New Testament, true obedience is ultimately determined not by a person's success in obeying the injunctions of the law, but by his faithful compliance with the demands of the gospel. *Consequently, the truly obedient are those who, having done their best to live as is worthy of the sons and daughters of God in Christ, recognize their sinfulness, imperfection, and unworthiness, and approach the Father in repentance and faith so that Christ's atoning blood may cleanse them of their guilt and His saving righteousness may keep them in a right standing with God.*

In view of this, it is also logical to say that when the biblical writer states that Jesus is "the source of eternal salvation for all who obey him" (Heb. 5:9), he does not refer to a hypothetical group of superachievers who through their flawless obedience to the law develop in their own lives a righteousness as complete and meritorious as that of Christ. Instead, the writer speaks of those obedient to the Saviour as He confronts them in the gospel—namely the believers of all ages who "obey the gospel of our Lord Jesus" (2 Thess. 1:8) in the fullest sense of the expression.

Although different in phraseology, the basic elements we have derived from Scripture are essentially the same as those we have seen earlier in Ellen White's writings: 1. Perfect obedience is possible only through repentance toward God on account of our sin and through faith in Christ for saving righteousness. 2. When we respond to the gospel in repentance and faith and come to the Father, trusting in the merits of the Son, our divine High Priest imputes the benefits of His redemptive work to us in order to make up for our deficiencies and to present us to God perfectly righteous in Christ.

III Christ's Mediation the Only Way to Saving Righteousness for All

Another concept clearly set forth in Ellen White's writings is that all fallen beings depend equally on Christ's mediation for a proper standing with God. No sinner has ever succeeded either in developing perfect righteousness of being or in living without sinning. Therefore all must avail themselves of Christ's atoning death, redemptive victory, and imputed righteousness for salvation.

1. Perfect Righteousness Never Achieved by Anyone Outside of Christ

The pen of inspiration, true to its task, tells us of the sins that overcame Noah, Lot, Moses, Abraham, David, and Solomon, and that even Elijah's strong spirit sank under temptation during his fearful trial. . . . The failings and infirmities of the prophets and apostles are all laid bare by the Holy Ghost, who lifts the veil from the human heart. There before us lie the lives of the believers, with all their faults and follies, which are intended as a lesson to all the generations following them. If they had been without foible they would have been more than human, and our sinful natures would despair of ever reaching such a point of excellence *(Testimonies, vol. 4, p. 12).*

He who bears with him a continual sense of the presence of Christ cannot indulge in self-confidence or self-righteousness. None of the prophets or apostles made proud boasts of holiness. The nearer they came to perfection of character, the less worthy and righteous they viewed themselves. But those who have the least sense of the perfection of Jesus, those whose eyes are least directed to Him, are the ones who make the strongest claim to perfection *(Faith and Works,* p. 54).

We may always be startled and indignant when we hear a poor, fallen mortal exclaiming, "I am holy; I am sinless!" Not one soul to whom God has granted the wonderful view of His greatness and majesty has ever uttered one word like this. On the contrary, they have felt like sinking down in the deepest humiliation of soul, as they have viewed the purity of God, and contrasted with it their own imperfections of life and character. . . . When the Spirit of Christ stirs the heart with its marvelous awakening power, there is a sense of deficiency in the soul, that leads to contrition of mind, and humiliation of self, rather than to proud boasting of what has been acquired (Ellen G. White, in *Review and Herald,* Oct. 16, 1888).

Those who experience the sanctification of the Bible will manifest a spirit of humility. Like Moses, they have had a view of the awful majesty of holiness, and they see their own unworthiness in contrast with the purity and exalted perfection of the Infinite One.

The prophet Daniel was an example of true sanctification. His long life was filled up with noble service for his Master. He was a man "greatly beloved" (Dan. 10:11) of Heaven. Yet instead of claiming to be pure and holy, this honored prophet identified himself with the really sinful of Israel as he pleaded before God in behalf of his people: "We do not present our supplications before thee for our righteousnesses, but for thy great mercies." "We have sinned, we have done wickedly." He declares: "I was speaking, and praying, and confessing my sin and the sin of my people." And when at a later time the Son of God appeared, to give him instruction, Daniel says: "My comeliness was turned in me into corruption, and I retained no strength" (Dan. 9:18, 15, 20; 10:8) *(The Great Controversy,* pp. 470, 471).

"If we," says John, not separating himself from his brethren, "say that we have no sin, we deceive ourselves, and the truth is not in us" (1 John 1:8) *(The Acts of the Apostles,* p. 562). Enoch was a man of strong and highly cultivated mind and extensive knowledge; he was honored with special revelations from God; yet being in constant communion with Heaven, with a sense of the divine greatness and perfection ever before him, he was one of the humblest of men. The closer the connection with God, the deeper was the sense of his own weakness and imperfection *(Patriarchs and Prophets,* p. 85).

No man can look within himself and find anything in his character that will recommend him to God, or make his acceptance sure. It is only through Jesus, whom the Father gave for the life of the world, that the sinner may find access to God. Jesus alone is our Redeemer, our Advocate and Mediator; in Him is our only hope for pardon, peace, and righteousness *(Selected Messages,* book 1, pp. 332, 333).

The preceding statements describe the experience of the patriarchs, prophets, and apostles—the spiritual giants of Scripture—who had a better chance than anyone else to develop flawless righteousness of being and to learn to live without sinning. Yet (1) none of them reached the goal of unblemished perfection on their own; (2) they all admitted being sinful, imperfect, and unworthy; and (3) they all depended on the imputed righteousness of Christ for salvation. Their admission of guilt and sinfulness did not result from a false sense of modesty or an inability to recognize their true spiritual standing. Instead, it rested on the fact that their unusually close relationship with God enabled them to acquire both the point of reference and the spiritual perception they needed to see themselves *as they really were.*

It would be difficult to argue convincingly that the apostles and prophets did not achieve the goal of sinlessness either because God did not give them sufficient divine power or because they did not try hard and long enough. On the contrary, we will see from *The Acts of the Apostles* that they were men "whom God . . . honored with divine light and power" and who "lived the nearest to God, men who would sacrifice life itself rather than knowingly commit a wrong act." So if anyone ever had the opportunity to achieve sinless perfection, they were the ones.

It is important to note that these spiritual giants recognized their total dependence on Christ for salvation, not so much because their obedience was deficient and they occasionally engaged in sinful behavior, but primarily because they had come to see the fallen condition in which they found themselves as individual persons. They knew that it was their spiritual imperfection, their defective character, their sinful nature, that made them unrighteous and rendered them unworthy.

> When the servant of God is permitted to behold the glory of the God of heaven, as He is unveiled to humanity, and realizes to a slight degree the purity of the Holy One of Israel, he will make startling confessions of *the pollution of his soul,* rather than proud boasts of his holiness. . . . One ray of the glory of God, one gleam of the purity of Christ, penetrating the soul, makes every spot of defilement painfully distinct, and lays bare the deformity and defects of the human character (Ellen G. White, in *Review and Herald,* Oct. 16, 1888; italics supplied).

None of the apostles and prophets ever claimed to be without sin. Men who have lived the nearest to God, men who would sacrifice life itself rather than knowingly commit a wrong act, men whom God has honored with divine light and power, have confessed *the sinfulness of their nature*. They have put no confidence in the flesh, have claimed no righteousness of their own, but have trusted wholly in the righteousness of Christ *(The Acts of the Apostles,* p. 561; italics supplied).

Ellen White gives great emphasis and significance to the fact that the believer's soul is polluted and his human nature sinful. One could even say that she considered it the single most important reason no fallen being is able to either render perfect obedience to the law or develop a righteousness God can accept. It also clarifies further why all fallen beings are equally dependent on Christ's mediation as their representative and substitute. The following passage explains this quite forcefully:

The religious services, the prayers, the praise, the penitent confession of sin ascend *from true believers* as incense to the heavenly sanctuary, but passing through *the corrupt channels of humanity,* they are so defiled that unless purified by blood, they can never be of value with God. They ascend not in spotless purity, and unless the Intercessor, who is at God's right hand, presents and purifies all by His righteousness, it is not acceptable to God. All incense from earthly tabernacles must be moist with the cleansing drops of the blood of Christ. He holds before the Father the censer of His own merits, in which there is no taint of earthly corruption. He gathers into this censer the prayers, the praise, and the confessions of His people, and with these He puts His own spotless righteousness. Then, perfumed with the merits of Christ's propitiation, the incense comes up before God wholly and entirely acceptable. Then gracious answers are returned.

Oh, that all may see that *everything in obedience, in penitence, in praise and thanksgiving, must be placed upon the glowing fire of the righteousness of Christ.* The fragrance of this righteousness ascends like a cloud around the mercy seat *(Selected Messages,* book 1, p. 344; italics supplied).

When we realize the far-reaching implications of the concepts expressed here, we begin to see that this passage holds the key to a correct understanding of at least two essential ideas that otherwise remain vague and ambiguous. That is, 1. That sinful beings cannot offer perfect obedience to God's will and therefore are unable to develop a righteous character on their own. 2. And that perfect obedience is only possible by partaking of the redemptive merits of Christ, by faith.

It was possible for Adam, before the fall, to form a righteous character by obedience to God's law. But he failed to do this, and because of his sin *our natures are fallen* and we cannot make ourselves righteous. Since we are sinful, unholy, we cannot perfectly obey the holy law. We have no righteousness of our own with which to meet the claims of the law of God *(Steps to Christ,* p. 62; italics supplied). The law demands righteousness, and this the sinner owes to the law; but he is incapable of rendering it *(Selected Messages,* book 1, p. 367). It [the law] could not justify man, because *in his sinful nature* he could not keep the law *(Patriarchs and Prophets,* p. 373; italics supplied).

If the law extended to the outward conduct only, men would not be guilty in their wrong thoughts, desires, and designs. But *the law requires that the soul itself be pure and the mind holy,* that the thoughts and feelings may be in accordance with the standard of love and righteousness *(Selected Messages,* book 1, p. 211; italics supplied). Man cannot meet the demands of that holy law without exercising repentance toward God and faith toward our Lord Jesus Christ *(Faith and Works,* p. 29).

We should notice several points here: 1. Man cannot perfectly obey the law because he is sinful—his sinful nature makes it impossible. Again, the issue is perfect obedience, an obedience God can accept on its own merit, without Christ's mediation. 2. Man does not have—nor is he able to develop—a personal righteousness capable of meeting the claims of the holy law. 3. The law covers not just what a person does but also what he is—it "requires that the soul itself be pure." That is, the law demands nothing less than total sinlessness of being and perfect righteousness of conduct.

The passage quoted from page 62 of *Steps to Christ* clearly indicates a radical difference between the initial possibilities of Adam and those of his fallen descendants. Notice again:

> It was possible for Adam, before the fall, to form a righteous character by obedience to God's law. But . . . our natures are fallen and we cannot make ourselves righteous. . . . We cannot perfectly obey the holy law.

If we take the passage literally—and there is no reason we should not—then we must conclude that, according to Ellen White, Adam could do at least two things that we, his fallen descendants cannot: First, he could render perfect obedience to God's law. And second, he could develop a righteous character by perfectly obeying God's law.

The cause-effect relationship that undergirds this argument actually has three basic parts, and we must consider all three if we are to properly understand it. 1. As a being created in God's image, Adam began his life with a nature that was righteous, holy, and good, and consequently he enjoyed God's absolute approval without the need of a mediator. 2. Since his nature was pure and sin-free and he lived in unhindered spiritual union with God—a branch perfectly connected to the Vine—he could live in complete harmony with God's will at all times and in every single respect. 3. Since he was righteous in himself, by nature, and consequently could offer perfect obedience, he could also develop a righteous character—a character that, because of its flawless quality, could receive God's full approval based on its own intrinsic merits.

Our situation is quite different, however. "Because of [Adam's] sin our natures are fallen. . . . Since we are sinful, unholy, we cannot perfectly obey the holy law." And since a righteous character can be formed only through *perfect obedience,* it logically follows that we cannot develop a righteous character as Adam could have—a character so intrinsically good, holy, and perfect that it would earn God's verdict of acceptance without the mediation of Christ.

Such considerations help us to draw at least two logical and significant conclusions: 1. Only sinless beings—those who do not have a sinful nature to defile and pollute everything they are and do—can live the type of lives and form the characters that will earn God's favorable verdict entirely on the basis of their own merits. 2. The only way in which any fallen being can satisfy God's standard of sinless perfection is through "repentance toward God and faith toward our Lord Jesus Christ." Only thus is his condemnation revoked and his sin removed. And only thus does he become a partaker of Christ's all-sufficient righteousness—the only righteousness in the universe available to fallen beings that meets God's standard of flawless perfection in all respects.

This understanding reinforces the significance of other passages that indicate that it is only the imputed righteousness of Christ—His unblemished character accepted in place of our imperfection—that qualifies us to stand pure and blameless in the presence of God. Notice:

You are powerless to do good, and cannot better your condition. Apart from Christ we have no merit, no righteousness. Our sinfulness, our weakness, our human imperfection make it impossible that we should appear before God unless we are clothed in Christ's spotless righteousness. We are to be found in Him not having our own righteousness, but the righteousness which is in Christ *(Selected Messages,* book 1, p. 333). Christ perfected a righteous character here upon the earth, not on His own account, for His character was pure and spotless, but for fallen man. His character He offers to man if he will accept it *(Testimonies,* vol. 3, p. 371).

Jesus says:

I will be your representative in heaven. The Father beholds not your faulty character, but He sees you as clothed in My perfection. I am the medium through which Heaven's blessings shall come to you. And everyone who confesses Me by sharing My sacrifice for the lost shall be confessed as a sharer in the glory and joy of the redeemed *(The Desire of Ages,* p. 357). Those who reject the gift of Christ's righteousness are rejecting the attributes of character which would constitute them the sons and daughters of God. They are rejecting that which alone could give them a fitness for a place at the marriage feast *(Christ's Object Lessons,* pp. 316, 317).

He lived a sinless life. He died for us, and now He offers to take our sins and give us His righteousness. If you give yourself to Him, and accept Him as your Saviour, then, sinful as your life may have been, for His sake you are accounted righteous. Christ's character stands in place of your character, and you are accepted before God just as if you had not sinned *(Steps to Christ,* p.

62). Christ imputes to us His sinless character, and presents us to the Father in His own purity (Ellen G. White, in *Review and Herald*, July 12, 1892).

Some believe that a sinner can live a sinless life by properly using the power of the Holy Spirit. Apparently they fail to see that the idea of a sinful being living a sinless life is in itself a contradiction of terms. The passage from *Selected Messages*, book 1, page 344, quoted earlier clearly indicates that even if a fallen being were able to perform in harmony with what God has stipulated—in his worship and obedience to the law—the "corrupt channels" of his sinful humanity would pollute all he does and render it unacceptable without Christ's mediation.

Because "our natures are fallen" and "we are sinful, unholy," even the good works we perform bear the incriminatory marks of our personal sinfulness. *Our worship and praise, our obedience and service, and our character development and behavior modification are all the works of sinful beings, and nothing sinful beings render to God is acceptable on its own merits*. It is only when we avail ourselves of Christ's mediation on our behalf, and He purifies and perfects all through the imputation of His personal merits, that our offering has access to the Father. The following passage underlines the fact that even *the good works of man* are worthless unless covered with Christ's merits:

> Although the good works of man are of no more value without faith in Jesus than was the offering of Cain, yet covered with the merit of Christ, they testify [to] the worthiness of the doer to inherit eternal life *(Selected Messages*, book 1, p. 382).

A second concept the passage from *Selected Messages*, book 1, page 344, quoted earlier helps us to understand more fully is the idea that perfect obedience is possible through union with Christ—by partaking of the divine nature, by combining humanity with divinity. Notice how Mrs. White explains this concept elsewhere:

> In order to meet the requirements of the law, our faith must grasp the righteousness of Christ, accepting it as our righteousness. *Through union with Christ,* through acceptance of His righteousness by faith, we may be qualified to work the works of God, to be colaborers with Christ *(ibid.,* p. 374; italics supplied). Christ came not to destroy but to fulfill the law. Not one jot or tittle of God's moral standard could be changed to meet man in his fallen condition. Jesus died that He might ascribe unto the repenting sinner His own righteousness, and make it possible for man to keep the law *(ibid.,* p. 312).

> All that man can do without Christ is polluted with selfishness and sin; but that which is wrought through faith is acceptable to God. When we seek to gain heaven through the merits of Christ, the soul makes progress. "Looking unto Jesus the author and finisher of our faith," we may go on from strength to strength, from victory to victory; for through Christ the grace of God has worked out our complete salvation *(Faith and Works,* p. 94).

> Christ took upon Himself humanity for us. He clothed His divinity, and divinity and humanity were combined. He showed that the law which Satan declared could not be kept could be kept. Christ took humanity to stand here in our world, to show that Satan had lied. He took humanity upon Himself to demonstrate that with *divinity and humanity combined,* man could keep the law of Jehovah. Separate humanity from divinity, and you can try to work out your own righteousness from now till Christ comes, and it will be nothing but a failure *(ibid.,* p. 71; italics supplied).

Satan had claimed that it was impossible for man to obey God's commandments; and in our own strength it is true that we cannot obey them. But Christ came in the form of humanity, and by His perfect obedience He proved that *humanity and divinity combined can obey every one of God's precepts (Christ's Object Lessons,* p. 314; italics supplied).

We must center our hopes of heaven upon Christ alone, because He is our Substitute and Surety. We have transgressed the law of God, and by the deeds of the law shall no flesh be justified. The best efforts that man in his own strength can make are valueless to meet the holy and just law that he has transgressed; but through faith in Christ he may claim the righteousness of the Son of God as all- sufficient. Christ satisfied the demands of the law in His human nature. He bore the curse of the law for the sinner, made an atonement for him, "that whosoever believeth in him should not perish, but have everlasting life." *Genuine faith appropriates the righteousness of Christ, and the sinner is made an overcomer with Christ; for he is made a partaker of the divine nature, and thus divinity and humanity are combined (Faith and Works,* pp. 93, 94; italics supplied).

God has plainly stated that He expects us to be perfect, and because He expects this, He has made provision for us to be partakers of the divine nature (Ellen G. White, in *Review and Herald,* Jan. 28, 1904). The gospel of Christ alone can free him [the transgressor] from the condemnation or the defilement of sin. *He must exercise repentance toward God, whose law has been transgressed; and faith in Christ, his atoning sacrifice. Thus he obtains "remission of sins that are past" and becomes a partaker of the divine nature (The Great Controversy,* p. 468; italics supplied).

A contextual examination of these statements clearly reveals that they do not refer to something belonging to the dimension of concrete physical reality. Instead, they speak of a spiritual phenomenon that is real only in the realm of faith. Consequently, we should not take expressions such as "union with Christ," "divinity and humanity combined," and "partaker of the divine nature" as references either to a pantheistic mixing of God and man or to a mystical blending of divine and human identities. The phrases are not suggesting a supernatural integration of human and divine natures, or some form of human deification. Instead, they speak about the believer becoming a faith participant in the Saviour's atoning death, redemptive victory, and all-sufficient righteousness.

"Union with Christ" takes place as our faith grasps "the righteousness of Christ, accepting it as our righteousness." "Divinity and humanity are combined" when "genuine faith appropriates the righteousness of Christ." The believer "becomes a partaker of the divine nature" when—and by reason of the fact that—he exercises "faith in Christ, his atoning sacrifice." Clearly, the righteousness of Christ is not a spiritual substance or a moral element that somehow gets infused into the believer. Instead, it is an intrinsic quality of Christ's own holy character—a merit, a value, a virtue—that He, as man's representative and substitute, can share with or impute to those who by faith accept Him as personal Saviour.

We therefore conclude that assertions such as "Humanity and divinity combined can obey every one of God's precepts" point to the same dynamics we studied earlier, namely that perfect obedience is possible only through Christ's mediation. When the believer does his best to live in harmony with what he knows of God's will for man and depends on Christ's redemptive work on his behalf for his standing with God, Christ imputes His personal righteousness to him and thus presents him and his performance perfectly acceptable to the Father.

2. How Christ Secures Eternal Salvation for Those Who Died Depending on God's Grace for Salvation.

We have seen that, according to Ellen White, none of the spiritual giants of biblical times—which really means absolutely no one—ever reached a state of sinless perfection on their own. They were all sinful, imperfect, unworthy, and hence totally dependent on Christ's imputed righteousness. Also, we have seen that none of them of themselves rendered flawless obedience. Besides being sinful and imperfect, their life performance was defiled and rendered unacceptable by the polluting effect of their inherent sinful nature. All they were, all they had, and all they did bore the incriminatory marks of their fallen state and personal sinfulness. Therefore, we face two questions: 1. Since they achieved neither righteousness of being nor sinlessness of conduct, will they be saved? 2. And if so, on what basis?

The following passage from Ellen White's pen answers both questions in a direct, clear, and sufficiently comprehensive way. It is part of a discussion of what in Adventist terminology we refer to as the investigative judgment, a judgment that, for believers that are not alive when Christ returns, will take place after their death, when it is too late for them to do anything to affect God's decision. At this judgment God's final and irreversible verdict permanently seals each person's eternal destiny. Among other things, the passage shows why the mediation of Christ is so essential for those who died trusting in His redemptive work.

> While Jesus is pleading for the subjects of His grace, Satan accuses them before God as transgressors. . . . He points to the record of their lives, to the defects of

character, the unlikeness to Christ, which has dishonored their Redeemer, to all the sins that he has tempted them to commit, and because of these he claims them as his subjects. Jesus does not excuse their sins, but shows their penitence and faith, and, claiming for them forgiveness, He lifts His wounded hands before the Father and the holy angels, saying: I know them by name. I have graven them on the palms of My hands. "The sacrifices of God are a broken spirit: a broken and a contrite heart, O God, thou wilt not despise" (Ps. 51:17). And to the accuser of His people He declares: "The Lord rebuke thee, O Satan; even the Lord that hath chosen Jerusalem rebuke thee: is not this a brand plucked out of the fire?" (Zech. 3:2). Christ will clothe His faithful ones with His own righteousness, that He may present them to His Father "a glorious church, not having spot, or wrinkle, or any such thing" (Eph. 5:27). Their names stand enrolled in the book of life, and concerning them it is written: "They shall walk with me in white: for they are worthy" (Rev. 3:4).

Thus will be realized the complete fulfillment of the new-covenant promise: "I will forgive their iniquity, and I will remember their sin no more." "In those days, and in that time, saith the Lord, the iniquity of Israel shall be sought for, and there shall be none; and the sins of Judah, and they shall not be found" (Jer. 31:34; 50:20) *(The Great Controversy,* pp. 484, 485).

Notice several significant details: 1. The passage describes a scene of judgment that forever establishes the eternal destiny of the subjects of Christ's grace—those who lived and died depending on God's grace for salvation. 2. The record of their lives shows that they did not achieve the goal of sinless perfection during their lifetime—their "defects of character" and "unlikeness to Christ" make that obvious enough. 3. Jesus does not question the accuracy of Satan's many accusations, nor does He argue that the accused eventually developed righteous characters and learned to live without sinning. 4. In their defense, Jesus points to their repentance and faith—the only response deemed acceptable—and that enables Christ to intercede actively in their behalf.

5. Lifting His wounded hands as a witness to His atoning death on their behalf, Jesus covers them with His own righteousness and thus presents them to the Father as a spotless, wrinkle-free, and glorious church. 6. Their names remain in the book of life, and God declares them to be worthy, not because of what they actually were or did during their lifetime, but because the merits of Christ cover them and make up for their deficiency. God pronounces them righteous in Christ, by faith, in spite of the fact that they still were sinful in themselves, by nature, and consequently failed to meet the standard of sinless perfection He requires.

7. Thus the gospel promise comes to full realization to those whom Paul so fittingly calls "the dead in Christ" (1 Thess. 4:16). That is, their destiny is sealed, their case is permanently closed. They will inherit eternal life, thanks to their faith in Christ's redemptive work on their behalf. Because they lived in a state of repentance and faith in Christ, their Mediator secured their forgiveness and covered them in His own imputed righteousness and thus made their salvation sure. When God will finally establish His eternal kingdom of glory, He will raise them back to life so that they may take their place among the redeemed of all ages.

This passage from *The Great Controversy* also helps us to see that Satan has his own conception of justice, his own standard by which a fallen being can become worthy of salvation, his own version of the gospel. According to this passage, Satan claims these people as his subjects for three basic reasons: their defective characters, their unlikeness to Christ, and their sinful behavior. It is therefore reasonable to conclude that if the record of their lives showed that they had developed flawless characters, that they had achieved Christlikeness, and that they had learned to live without sinning, Satan would yield—he would recognize that they are worthy of salvation.

Note three details in Satan's theology of salvation: 1. His method centers on works, performance, or achievement. He wants every person to be rewarded according to what he deserves, based on his own achievements. The devil wants God to determine each individual's eternal destiny on the basis of his actual, objective life record. 2. Each person's relationship to sin is the decisive factor. If he somehow has been involved in sin, then God must execute the penalty—he is worthy of death, so death must be his fate.

3. Satan's method has no room for either grace or faith. *It decides the destiny of sinners as though there were no Saviour.* The atoning death, redemptive victory, and saving righteousness of Christ make no difference here. What Jesus did yesterday as our substitute throughout His earthly life, and particularly on the cross, and what He is doing for us today as our representative with the Father on the throne, play absolutely no role in Satan's plan. All that counts takes place in our present historical lives. Either we show we have a righteous character, like Jesus' character, and demonstrate we can live without sinning, like Jesus did, or else we are forever lost.

It should come as no surprise that Satan has incorporated some elements of God's plan of redemption into his own. Counterfeits always resemble the original to some degree, and deceptions never depart totally from the truth they distort. In both plans the law functions as the standard to evaluate a person's conduct.

Both plans hold up Jesus Christ as the ultimate example of what it means to be truly righteous, good, and holy— of what the Creator intended man should be. And each has a judgment that reviews a person's life and decides his eternal destiny.

When we examine the similarities and consider the differences, however, we soon discover that while Satan has incorporated what God demands of us, he has left out the provision God has made in Christ. Satan likes the law, not because it provides the basic standard by which we can distinguish what is true and good and loving from what is sinful, but because it condemns us all as transgressors.

Satan does not use the concept of Jesus as our example because He provides a revelation of what God's character is truly like, and of what man—initially created in the image of God—would be like if sin had not perverted his spiritual wholeness and moral perfection. Rather, he stresses Jesus as the model because he knows that nothing will make our sinfulness, imperfection, and unworthiness more obvious and render our case more hopeless than an unmediated comparison between ourselves and Christ.

The enemy also welcomes the judgment, not because there God's grace finds its glory as Jesus absolves our condemnation and declares us righteous in Himself (see Rom. 3:21-26). Instead, he wants us to face the judgment because he knows we are guilty. If he could have us rewarded for what we are, what we have, and what we do, our condemnation is assured.

The passage from *The Great Controversy* shows that God's plan of redemption is different from Satan's theology in all three major areas just listed: 1. God's program of salvation is not achievement-centered but Christ-centered. According to God's plan, the believer has his destiny ultimately determined, not by how good he is, how much righteousness he has developed, or how many temptations he has successfully overcome, but by his faith-participation in Christ's redemptive work.

2. In God's system, what is decisive is not a person's involvement with sin, but his relationship to the Saviour. With God the real question is not "What have you done about sin?" but "What have you done with Jesus Christ and the salvation He provided for sinners just like you?" According to God's plan, the crucial issue is whether or not the sinner responded to the gospel in repentance and faith, and in so doing, obtained access to both God's forgiveness for his sin and Christ's imputed righteousness to make up for his spiritual inadequacy and moral imperfection.

3. Contrary to Satan's counterfeit, God's plan of redemption makes grace and faith central. By grace God provides for man's sin problem a solution that bestows forgiveness and saving righteousness through the redemptive work of Christ on man's behalf. And both forgiveness and righteousness are accessible to the sinner only through repentance and faith. God can forgive the repentant sinner only because Christ's redemptive work is both atoning and substitutionary. And the sinner can partake in the redemptive activity of Christ—he can benefit from it, he can avail himself of it—only as his faith lays hold of Christ as his personal Saviour.

This comparison/contrast helps us see the radical difference between God's program of salvation and Satan's counterfeit. In the counterfeit everything revolves around the sinner and his personal accomplishments. His eternal destiny ultimately depends on what he is in himself—whether he is spiritually perfect or imperfect. What he has—whether it is personal merit or guilt. And what he does—whether it is morally righteous or sinful. Satan claims that all who have "defects of character," who show "unlikeness to Christ," and who have engaged in sinful behavior are "his subjects," and therefore deserve not everlasting life but eternal destruction.

In contrast, the gospel makes everything revolve around Christ and the sinner's response to Him. When it is time to decide the eternal destiny of "the subjects of His grace,"

> Jesus does not excuse their sins, but shows their penitence and faith, and, claiming for them forgiveness, He lifts His wounded hands before the Father. . . . Christ will clothe His faithful ones with His own righteousness, that He may present them to His Father "a glorious church, not having spot, or wrinkle, or any such thing" (Eph. 5:27). . . . Thus will be realized the complete fulfillment of the new-covenant promise.

3. Some Scriptural Considerations

The fact that all believers equally depend on Christ's mediation for both forgiveness and saving righteousness is graphically illustrated by Israel's experience as God's people. Their special relationship with God began when He acted in their behalf by delivering them from captivity and granting them freedom. The basis on which God chose them as His people was not their own goodness, righteousness, or merits—for they had none—but the love and faithfulness of the covenant-keeping God (Deut. 9:5-7; 7:7-9).

Their participation in His redemptive act set them apart as His personal people to enjoy a special relationship with Him and to be holy unto Him. Shortly after their deliverance, God sealed their covenant relationship by giving them two separate yet interrelated institutions, namely the law and the sanctuary. The law's most obvious function consisted of prescribing the conduct of those God had redeemed and sanctified. The law regulated their relationship with Him, with one another, with other peoples, and with the inheritance God was going to give them to enjoy and to administer as His stewards.

Obedience to God's law was a blessing in itself. It enabled the Israelites to live peacefully and productively and made them a holy, happy, and healthy people. But God's law was more than an effective way to enrich their lives: it was a test of loyalty to their Redeemer, as well. For God's people, His commands and precepts were not optional, but mandatory. In fact, they constituted the standard that determined an Israelite's right to continue as a covenant member of God's people. Violations of God's law could result in being cut off from the community of Israel (Num. 15:30, 31), or even in death (Ex. 21:14).

The law's less obvious, yet equally significant, function was to serve as a continuous reminder to Israel that they had not earned the right to be God's people, and did not deserve the special status-relationship He had placed them in. Their constant failure to perfectly obey the law showed again and again that all they were and all to which they had access was, and would always be, not a right earned through a flawless observance of the law, but a gift of God's grace mediated through the sanctuary in the form of forgiveness.

When God gave them His law, the Israelites solemnly promised to be "careful to obey all this law before the Lord our God" (Deut. 6:25; cf. Ex. 19:8; 24:3, 7). And they meant it. We have no reason to believe that they were not honest in their resolve. After all, they had accepted God's redemption and were enjoying a privileged status/relationship with Him as His people. But God realized He could not make the perpetuation of His covenant dependent on their good intentions.

God knew His people's "frame" and remembered that they were "dust," as David puts it (Ps. 103:14, RSV). He saw that "the spirit" of His children "is willing, but the flesh is weak," as Jesus said (Matt. 26:41, RSV). God understood their willingness, but He provided a covenant adapted to their great need and limited potential. And so He gave them the sanctuary, also. "Have them make a sanctuary for me, and I will dwell among them," He told Moses (Ex. 25:8).

The sanctuary was for Old Testament times what the gospel is for the New. The services that took place there symbolized Christ and His sacrificial-mediatorial ministry—the ministry through which He provides both forgiveness and righteousness for those who accept Him by faith. The sanctuary granted atonement to those who, in spite of their resolve to be faithful to God and the gracious covenant He had made with them, found themselves guilty of disloyalty; those who, although they had seriously attempted to obey the law of God, had violated it nevertheless; and those who, having recognized their unfaithfulness, repented of their sin and in faith brought to God the sacrifice He had stipulated.

The main features of the administration of justice through the sanctuary were as follows: Whenever someone violated God's law, he became "guilty. When he [was] made aware of the sin he committed" (Lev. 4:27, 28)—through the convicting of the Spirit (John 16:7, 8)—he had to "confess in what way he [had] sinned" and bring a "sin offering" to the sanctuary (Lev. 5:5). After he killed the sacrifice (Lev. 4:29), the priest made "atonement for him," and he was "forgiven" (verse 31).

The sanctuary provided forgiveness for the "anointed priest," for the "leader" ("ruler," RSV) of the people, and for the common "member of the community" alike (verses 3, 22, 27). And *all depended on this forgiveness for their continued participation in God's covenant with Israel.* We cannot consider even the high priests an exception, for, according to Scripture, "every high priest" "is beset with weakness. Because of this he is bound to offer sacrifice for his own sins as well as for those of the people" (Heb. 5:1-3, RSV; cf. Lev. 16:3-6).

To be forgiven meant that the punishment God had pronounced on the transgressor of the law did not fall on the sinner. He was not cut off, but remained a member of God's people in good and regular standing—just as if he had not violated the law at all. True, he had sinned and was guilty of breaking his covenant with God, and yet He treated him just as if he had been faithful—as if he had kept the law with absolute flawlessness—thanks to the provision of forgiveness God had made available through the sanctuary.

Under this Old Testament arrangement, the sanctuary functioned as a courthouse, or judgment hall, where God decided whether or not a particular individual continued to belong to the community of His people. Since no Israelite ever succeeded in rendering perfect obedience, the law rightfully condemned all Israelites as equally guilty and undeserving. But if they availed themselves of the atonement provided, the sanctuary overruled the condemnation of the law. It replaced the law's verdict of guilty, based on their personal works, with one of justified, or nonguilty, grounded on God's forgiving grace. Consequently it was an Israelite's relationship to the sanctuary that ultimately decided his fate, for it was the sanctuary—not the law—that had the final word concerning his personal standing with God.

SAVING RIGHTEOUSNESS FOR ALL

The provision of forgiveness through the sanctuary was essential for Israel's continued existence as God's people. Had He not planted the sanctuary in the middle of the camp, the Israelites would have lost their special covenant relationship with God long before they reached the borders of the Promised Land. And throughout their later history, at no time did their status-relationship as God's people not ultimately depend on the provision He had made available to them through the services that prefigured the redemptive role of Christ.

What was true for Israel as a people was also true for each one of its individual members. Nowhere does Scripture speak of someone in the nation's long and varied history who ever occupied his place among God's people on the basis of his perfect obedience to the law. As was the case with Paul, "the very commandment which promised life proved to be death" to them (Rom. 7:10, RSV), precisely because their obedience was at best partial and imperfect. That is why all of them—kings and judges, prophets and priests, and rich and poor alike—retained their membership in the community of Israel, thanks only to God's grace expressed through the sanctuary.

The provision was so complete that the Israelites had no need ever to lose their special covenant relationship with God. And yet that is precisely what happened to them as a nation. Slowly they shifted the basis of their assurance from God's grace as mediated through the sanctuary to some of the traditions and outstanding personalities of their religious heritage. They came to believe that because at one time God had chosen them they would remain His special people forever.

Their dependence on obedience to the law for a right standing with God eventually became so all-inclusive that when Jesus came preaching repentance from sin and faith in His substitutionary death (see Mark 1:14, 15; Heb. 9:26-28; 1 Peter 1:18, 19; John 6:35), when He came to "save his people from their sins" (Matt. 1:21)—to take away, to atone for, to remove through His vicarious death, "the sin of the world" (John 1:29)—they passed Him by in favor of their own traditions.

The tragedy is that when they rejected the true atonement provided through the sacrifice of Jesus, on whom "the Lord has laid . . . the iniquity of us all," and who died as "an offering for sin" (Isa. 53:6, 10, RSV), God could do nothing more to retain them as His exclusive covenant people. *Evidently the Israelites lost their special covenant relationship with God and fell away from grace, not through their failure to provide perfect obedience to the law—God had made provision for that—but rather through their failure to accept Christ's atoning sacrifice, previously symbolized by the sanctuary and its services.*

It seems that to a large degree Israel's spiritual problem resulted from—and their destiny as a people was eventually determined by—a two-sided theological misunderstanding of man's real predicament as a sinner. They thought that only conscious violations of the letter of the law were sinful. That is why many spiritual leaders felt that only robbers, criminals, adulterers, and the like needed repentance and forgiveness. Apparently it never occurred to them that in spite of their intense religiosity and zealous concern for the law, they were spiritually destitute and morally imperfect and consequently required a Saviour just as much as the despised tax collectors, prostitutes, and other such open sinners.

Jesus told the Jews, "It is not the healthy who need a doctor, but the sick. I have not come to call the righteous, but sinners" (Mark 2:17). According to Scripture, "there is no one righteous, not even one" (Rom. 3:10; cf. Ps. 14:1-3). Therefore we should not interpret Christ's statement to mean that only some people are "sick" and require spiritual healing, or worse, that some are actually "righteous" and therefore do not need Him as their personal Saviour.

Instead, Jesus is revealing the fact that only those who recognize themselves to be sinners, those who are aware of their spiritual imperfection—the "poor in spirit," the ones who "mourn" on account of their sinfulness and seek God's "righteousness" (Matt. 5:3, 4; 6:33)—feel their need of a Saviour and avail themselves of Christ's redemptive work. "It is only he who knows himself to be a sinner that Christ can save. . . . We must know our real condition, or we shall not feel our need of Christ's help" (Christ's Object Lessons, p. 158).

In contrast, those who consider themselves righteous remain unaware of their spiritual difficulties and consequently do not depend on His redemptive work for their standing with God. As a result, Christ's atonement and mediation have no efficacy for them. Elsewhere Jesus explains in more detail the difference between those who recognize their spiritual need and those who don't:

> I tell you the truth, the tax collectors and the prostitutes are entering the kingdom of God ahead of you. For John came to you to show you the way of righteousness, and you did not believe him, but the tax collectors and the prostitutes did. And even after you saw this, you did not repent and believe (Matt. 21:31, 32).

Because the Jews defined sin only in terms of conscious acts that violated the letter of the law, they failed to see their personal sinfulness, which called for a Saviour. They did not realize that because they were imperfect and unworthy, they were as dependent on the merits of the atoning blood of Christ as were the tax collectors and the prostitutes, who lived in open sin. This misconception of the Jews eventually led them to personally reject Jesus as the "capstone" (verse 42) of their personal salvation. "Therefore," Jesus told them, "the kingdom of God will be taken away from you" (verse 43).

According to Jesus, then, such Jews did not lose their participation in God's kingdom of grace because they willfully neglected His law, consciously lived in open sin, or deliberately rebelled against God's rulership—for such was not the case. They forfeited it, rather, because in their religious self-sufficiency they "did not repent and believe" in order to secure the forgiveness and saving righteousness God made available in Christ. Consequently, they had no part in Christ's kingdom of grace and no right to eternal life.

Not all Israelites lost their covenant relationship with God, however. Some of those who kept it were Christ's early followers and most of the early church, who were Jewish. And when God will finally bring the covenant promises to full realization as He establishes His eternal kingdom of glory at the second coming of Christ, many Israelites will receive everything to which their covenant relationship with God entitles them. Speaking of those who based their hope on the coming Messiah and "were still living by faith when they died" (Heb. 11:13), Scripture states:

> These were all commended for their faith, yet none of them received what had been promised. God had planned something better for us so that only together with us would they be made perfect (verses 39, 40).

Notice particularly two details here: 1. All the spiritual giants of the Old Testament of which this passage speaks accomplished great feats for God—they all obtained a good report—but none of them before they died achieved sinless perfection during their lifetime. That is something that still awaits them in the future. 2. "None of them received what had been promised," but because they "were still living by faith when they died," they "gained approval through their faith" (NASB) and therefore will "be made perfect" together with all the redeemed of all times at the second coming of Jesus.

The experience of the Old Testament heroes of faith beautifully illustrates how God fulfills His redemptive word. The scriptural promise is that "whoever believes in [Jesus Christ] shall not perish but have eternal life" (John 3:16). Jesus claimed to be the only way: "No one comes to the Father except through me," He said (John 14:6). According to the prophetic promise of John 3:16, all those who live by faith in God's plan for the redemption of sinners will have eternal life. By the same token, all who refuse to place their faith in Christ's redemptive work as the only way to the Father will perish.

On the basis of such considerations, we conclude that all humans alike—from Abel, the first believer to die, to the last sinner to accept God's saving grace in Christ just before probation ends—depend equally on Christ's redemptive activity for salvation. Because all are sinful, imperfect, and unworthy, and God devised a plan of redemption according to which Jesus Christ is the only way to the Father, all humans will either be saved by grace or not at all.

According to Scripture, "there is no one righteous, not even one. . . . All have sinned and fall short of the glory of God" (Rom. 3:10-23). Therefore, either they must accept God's undeserved forgiveness, based on Christ's atoning death on their behalf, or they will stand guilty before the judgment bar of God. And either they accept the imputed righteousness of Christ, centered in the Saviour's substitutionary life, or they will remain in their state of lostness, spiritual destitution, and eventual death. Fallen man simply has no other options available.

IV The Mediation of Christ the Only Way to Saving Righteousness to the Very End

The writings of Ellen White also express the idea that all believers must have the righteousness of Christ for a right standing with God to the very end. The expression "to the very end" has a double application: It means, first, that those who die before the close of probation continue to rely on the mediation of Christ for salvation to the close of their lives. And second, that the last generation of believers—those living at the time when the world's probation closes, and consequently must face the pre-Advent judgment during their lifetime—need Christ's mediation, to secure God's final verdict of acceptance, as much as all the generations that preceded them.

1. A Progressively Intimate Relationship With God, Leading to a Deeper Awareness of Personal Sinfulness, and a Greater Reliance on Christ for Salvation

Common sense would seem to indicate that the longer a believer continues in the process of Christian growth, the closer he should find himself to achieving the goal of sinless perfection, and consequently the less he should need Christ's mediation for him. The consciousness of his sinfulness, imperfection, and unworthiness should decrease in somewhat direct proportion to his spiritual maturation, character development, and behavioral modification. Strange as it may seem, however, Ellen White rejects such a notion. Notice particularly that an individual's perception of his own spiritual condition—whether he sees himself as righteous and good or imperfect and sinful—is said to be determined by his relative spiritual closeness to Jesus and by the adequacy of his view of the perfection of Christ.

> The nearer we come to Jesus, and the more clearly we discern the purity of His character, the more clearly shall we see the exceeding sinfulness of sin, and the less shall we feel like exalting ourselves. There will be a continual reaching out of the soul after God, a continual, earnest, heartbreaking confession of sin and humbling of the heart before Him (*The Acts of the Apostles*, p. 561). There can be no self-exaltation, no boastful claim to freedom from sin, on the part of those who walk in the shadow of Calvary's cross. They feel that it was their sin which caused the agony that broke the heart of the Son of God, and this thought will lead them to self-abasement. Those who live nearest to Jesus discern most clearly the frailty and sinfulness of humanity, and [that] their only hope is in the merit of a crucified and risen Saviour (*The Great Controversy*, p. 471).

> Perfection through our own good works we can never attain. The soul who sees Jesus by faith repudiates his own righteousness. He sees himself as incomplete, his repentance insufficient, his strongest faith but feebleness, his most costly sacrifice as meager, and he sinks in humility at the foot of the cross (*Faith and Works*, p. 107). When we see Jesus, . . . self will no longer clamor to be recognized. Looking unto Jesus, we shall be ashamed of our coldness, our lethargy, our self-seeking (*The Desire of Ages*, p. 439).

> The closer you come to Jesus, the more faulty you will appear in your own eyes; for your vision will be clearer, and your imperfections will be seen in broad and distinct contrast to His perfect nature. This is evidence that

THE ONLY WAY TO SAVING RIGHTEOUSNESS

Satan's delusions have lost their power; that the vivifying influence of the Spirit of God is arousing you. No deep-seated love for Jesus can dwell in the heart that does not realize its own sinfulness. The soul that is transformed by the grace of Christ will admire His divine character; but if we do not see our own moral deformity, it is unmistakable evidence that we have not had a view of the beauty and excellence of Christ *(Steps to Christ,* pp. 64, 65).

Our love to Christ will be in proportion to the depth of our conviction of sin *(Faith and Works,* p. 96). But we must have a knowledge of ourselves, a knowledge that will result in contrition, before we can find pardon and peace. . . . It is only he who knows himself to be a sinner that Christ can save *(Christ's Object Lessons,* p. 158). When men see their own nothingness, they are prepared to be clothed with the righteousness of Christ *(The Faith I Live By,* p. 111).

And the claim to be without sin is, in itself, evidence that he who makes this claim is far from holy. It is because he has no true conception of the infinite purity and holiness of God or of what they must become who shall be in harmony with His character; because he has no true conception of the purity and exalted loveliness of Jesus, and the malignity and evil of sin, that man can regard himself as holy. The greater the distance between himself and Christ, and the more inadequate his conceptions of the divine character and requirements, the more righteous he appears in his own eyes *(The Great Controversy,* p. 473).

In one way only can a true knowledge of self be obtained. We must behold Christ. It is ignorance of Him that makes men so uplifted in their own righteousness. When we contemplate His purity and excellence, we shall see our own weakness and poverty and defects as they really are. We shall see ourselves lost and hopeless, clad in garments of self-righteousness, like every other sinner. We shall see that if we are ever saved, it will not be through our own goodness, but through God's infinite grace *(Christ's Object Lessons,* p. 159).

The true follower of Christ will make no boastful claims to holiness. It is by the law of God that the sinner is convicted. He sees his own sinfulness in contrast with the perfect righteousness which it enjoins, and this leads him to humility and repentance. He becomes reconciled to God through the blood of Christ, and as he continues to walk with Him he will be gaining a clearer sense of the holiness of God's character and the far-reaching nature of His requirements. He will see more clearly his own defects and will feel the need of continual repentance and faith in the blood of Christ *(Faith and Works,* pp. 53, 54).

These Ellen White statements describe the theological views, spiritual insights, and personal experiences of two radically different kinds of religious people. Those of the first group do not have a close and enlightened faith relationship with Jesus and consequently lack both the point of reference and the spiritual eyesight that would enable them to see their true predicament as fallen beings. They are religious moralists obviously concerned about achieving a sinless condition. Unfortunately they underestimate their sinfulness and overestimate their potential. As a result they do not sense that their total acceptance with God comes through Christ. They apparently view His mediation as a temporary arrangement intended to assist them until they achieve a state of flawlessness and learn to live without sinning.

Ellen White mentions several negative characteristics of this group: 1. They live at a great spiritual distance from Christ—apparently without realizing it. 2. Controlled by Satan's delusion of self-righteousness, they have not let the vivifying influence of the Holy Spirit arouse them. 3. Not having a clear view of Jesus' purity and loveliness, they believe that they can match His righteousness in their own personal lives. 4. Without a true conception of the divine requirements, they think they can fully satisfy them.

5. An inadequate conception of what they must become in order to be in harmony with the character of God causes them to underestimate how short they really fall of the divine standard. 6. They do not discern the frailty and sinfulness of humanity—which blinds them to the true depth of their spiritual wretchedness. 7. And they have a simplistic definition of sin, an inadequate understanding of its true malignity, which blinds them to the fact that only Christ can give them a right standing with God.

The second group consists of "the true followers of Christ," who live in a close and enlightened faith relationship with Him and are therefore spiritually sensitive. Having had a view of the purity and excellence of Jesus, they see their "own weakness and poverty and defects *as they really are*." That is why they repudiate their own righteousness, see themselves as incomplete, their repentance insufficient, their strongest faith as feebleness, and recognize that "their only hope is in the merit of a crucified and risen Saviour."

Those belonging to the second group exhibit at least the following traits: 1. They have come to appreciate the beauty of Christ's holy character. 2. They have a clear understanding of the far-reaching nature of God's requirements, of what they must become in order to meet the standard He has established. 3. They have an adequate conception of the terribleness of sin and of the frailty and sinfulness of humanity. 4. They recognize their personal sinfulness, inadequacy, and unworthiness. 5. They live in a state of "continual repentance and faith in the blood of Christ," fully aware that their salvation depends, not on their own goodness, but on God's infinite grace.

We can therefore say that the block of Ellen White passages quoted earlier in this chapter leads to at least four conclusions: First, the believer who maintains a healthy and growing faith relationship with Jesus Christ comes increasingly closer to the Saviour. Second, the closer he approaches Jesus, the more clearly he sees his own imperfection, sinfulness, and unworthiness. Third, his realization does not arise from either a false sense of modesty or a poor spiritual discernment. Instead, it is based (1) on his growing spiritual capacity to see himself as he really is—as God views him independently of the imputed righteousness of Christ—and (2) on his increasing perception of the absolute perfection of Christ. Fourth, the believer's progressive realization of his true spiritual inadequacy leads him to depend more and more on Christ until the end of his life.

2. The Experience of the Remnant Church

According to Ellen White, all true believers will continue living in a state of constant repentance on account of their sin, and faith in Jesus Christ for saving righteousness, to the very end of time. The following passage describes the experience of the last generation of believers as they face God's final judgment at the time when the world's probation comes to its conclusion. Among other things, it shows the decisive role Jesus plays as mediator.

> The fact that the acknowledged people of God are represented as standing before the Lord in filthy garments should lead to humility and deep searching of heart on the part of all who profess His name. Those who are indeed purifying their souls by obeying the truth will

have a most humble opinion of themselves. The more closely they view the spotless character of Christ, the stronger will be their desire to be conformed to His image, and the less will they see of purity or holiness in themselves. But while we should realize our sinful condition, we are to rely upon Christ as our righteousness, our sanctification, and our redemption. We cannot answer the charges of Satan against us. Christ alone can make an effectual plea in our behalf. He is able to silence the accuser with arguments founded not upon our merits, but on His own. . . .

Zechariah's vision of Joshua and the Angel applies with peculiar force to the experience of God's people in the closing up of the great day of atonement. The remnant church will be brought into great trial and distress. Those who keep the commandments of God and the faith of Jesus will feel the ire of the dragon and his hosts. . . .

As Joshua was pleading before the Angel, so the remnant church, with brokenness of heart and earnest faith, will plead for pardon and deliverance through Jesus their Advocate. They are fully conscious of the sinfulness of their lives, they see their weakness and unworthiness, and as they look upon themselves they are ready to despair. The tempter stands by to accuse them, as he stood by to resist Joshua. He points to their filthy garments, their defective characters. He presents their weakness and folly, their sins of ingratitude, their unlikeness to Christ, which has dishonored their Redeemer. . . .

The people of God are sighing and crying for the abominations done in the land. . . . And with unutterable sorrow they humble themselves before the Lord on account of their own transgressions. . . . It is because they are drawing nearer to Christ, and their eyes are fixed upon His perfect purity, that they so clearly discern the exceeding sinfulness of sin. Their contrition and self-abasement are infinitely more acceptable in the sight of God than is the self-sufficient, haughty spirit of those who see no cause to lament, who scorn the humility of Christ, and who claim perfection while transgressing God's holy law. Meekness and lowliness of heart are the conditions for strength and victory. The crown of glory awaits those who bow at the foot of the cross. Blessed are these mourners, for they shall be comforted. . . .

As the people of God afflict their souls before Him, pleading for purity of heart, the command is given, "Take away the filthy garments" from them, and the encouraging words are spoken, "Behold, I have caused thine iniquity to pass from thee, and I will clothe thee with change of raiment." The spotless robe of Christ's righteousness is placed upon the tried, tempted, yet faithful children of God. The despised remnant are clothed in glorious apparel, nevermore to be defiled by the corruptions of the world. Their names are retained in the Lamb's book of life, enrolled among the faithful of all ages (*Testimonies*, vol. 5, pp. 471-475).

The passage hardly needs any explanation. But in order to highlight its significance to the overall theme of our study, we will call attention to four points: First, the passage discusses the experience of "the acknowledged people of God," "the remnant church," at the time of the "closing up of the great day of atonement." That is to say, it sketches what will happen to the last generation of believers as God permanently and irreversibly decides their permanent destiny at the pre-Advent judgment.

Second, the passage clearly states that the remnant church does not reach sinless perfection of either being or conduct by the time probation ends. They are not supersaints who have fully attained and therefore stand in flawless righteousness before the tribunal of God. On the contrary, they are sinners who, save for Christ's righteousness, have nothing but "filthy garments" to wear. Painfully aware of "the sinfulness of their lives, . . . their weakness and unworthiness," "their defective characters," "their unlikeness to Christ," they "afflict their souls" in repentance before God "on account of their own transgressions," and plead for a "purity of heart" they obviously do not yet possess.

Third, if those believers alive when the pre-Advent judgment concludes had actually transcended their fallen condition, had developed flawless righteousness of being, had learned to live without sinning, then they would be able to answer Satan's charges against them. But that is most definitely not the case. The accused cannot answer his indictment because the charges against them are true. They are indeed guilty, imperfect, and sinful. That is precisely why "as they look upon themselves they are ready to despair." They have no basis for self-defense.

Should God determine their eternal destiny on the basis of their true spiritual condition and actual behavioral performance, their case would be hopeless. But then Jesus, the powerful mediator, makes an effectual plea on their behalf. He silences the accuser with arguments founded, not upon the believers' merits—for they have none—but upon His own. He credits, He applies, His merits to them on the basis of their faith in Him as their advocate before the Father.

Fourth, the final judgment of the remnant church comes to a permanent resolution when Jesus, the mediator, does two essential things on their behalf: 1. He commands that their filthy garments be removed from them—He causes their iniquity to pass from them and forgives their sin. 2. He covers them with the glorious robe of His own spotless righteousness—He imputes His personal righteousness to them so that they may be complete in Christ by faith. As a result, their names remain in the Lamb's book of life, enrolled among the faithful of all ages, never to be removed. Their judgment is now over, their cases forever closed, their eternal destiny permanently sealed.

Clearly, then, the mediation of Christ is as vital as His death on the cross for the last generation because without His imputed righteousness the remnant church would have nothing with which to counter Satan's charges against them, no righteousness with which to meet the standard God requires for salvation. That is what makes the following statements so pertinent:

> It is not God's will that you should be distrustful, and torture your soul with the fear that God will not accept you because you are sinful and unworthy. . . . Present your case before Him, pleading the merits of the blood shed for you upon Calvary's cross. Satan will accuse you of being a great sinner, and you must admit this, but you can say: "I know I am a sinner, and that is the reason I need a Saviour . . . I have no merit or goodness whereby I may claim salvation, but I present before God the all-atoning blood of the spotless Lamb of God, which taketh away the sin of the world. This is my only plea. The name of Jesus gives me access to the Father" (Ellen G. White, in *Signs of the Times,* July 4, 1892).

> If you would stand through the time of trouble, you must know Christ, and appropriate the gift of His righteousness, which He imputes to the repentant sinner (Ellen G. White, in *Review and Herald,* Nov. 22, 1892).

The requirement for salvation, and the way to achieve it, is the same from the beginning to the end of time. We will consider two points: First, *the last generation must meet the same standard of perfection as all those who went before*. Since God required total righteousness of being and flawless obedience to His will of all previous generations, that is precisely what He expects of the remnant church—the standard neither raises nor lowers for them.

Second, *the last generation will meet the standard and achieve the goal in the same way all previous generations did.* All those who lived before—including the giants of faith and the martyrs of all ages —were guilty, imperfect, and unworthy sinners, totally dependent on Christ for salvation. So it is with the true believers of the last days. God will save them, not on the basis of their unprecedented spiritual achievements, but because the Mediator removes their filthy garments—the partial and imperfect righteousness they developed in their own lives—and covers them with the robe of His all-sufficient righteousness. Thus Christ presents them to the Father as perfectly righteous in Him by faith.

Obviously we can find some significant similarities between those still living by faith in Christ when they died and those living by faith in Christ when probation closes: 1. Both groups, Ellen White says, are unworthy, imperfect, and sinful—she mentions their "unlikeness to Christ," their "defective characters." 2. Both groups stand guilty and helpless before God—they cannot counter Satan's charges because these accurately reflect who they really are and what they have actually done. 3. The judgment makes the eternal salvation of both groups permanently secure, not because they have achieved perfect spiritual wholeness and learned to live without sinning—for such is not the case—but because the Saviour applies the benefits of His redemptive victory to them and presents them to the Father as being righteous, holy, and worthy in Christ by faith.

3. Some Scriptural Considerations

The New Testament writers believed they were living near the close of human history. As far as they were concerned, they were the last generation of believers. A sense of urgency permeated their writings precisely because they felt that the day of the Lord was at hand. Therefore, we can consider most of what they wrote with their contemporaries in mind, with slight adaptations, as directly applicable to those living at the end-time.

As we examine the apostolic writings in search of something that might apply to those alive when Jesus returns, we find that they have three major concerns: 1. They warn the believers against giving up their faith, because in so doing they would lose their participation in the gospel promises. "By this gospel you are saved, if you hold firmly to the word I preached to you," says Paul. "Otherwise, you have believed in vain" (1 Cor. 15:2). 2. They encourage the believers to "live holy and godly lives" as they wait for the Advent (2 Peter 3:11, 12). 3. They urge them to continue in their faith "till the end" (Heb. 3:14) so that "the hope held out in the gospel" (Col. 1:23) may indeed become a reality to them.

Speaking about his own Christian experience, Paul said:

> I have fought the good fight, I have finished the race, I have kept the faith. Now there is in store for me the crown of righteousness, which the Lord, the righteous Judge, will award to me on that day—and not only to me, but also to all who have longed for his appearing (2 Tim. 4:7, 8).

First, let us note that Paul based his assurance of a "crown of righteousness" on the fact that he "fought the good fight," "finished the race," and "kept the faith."

THE ONLY WAY TO SAVING RIGHTEOUSNESS

Obviously he died as he had lived, depending not on his own merits and achievements but on "the righteousness that comes from God and is by faith" in Christ (Phil. 3:9). Second, the apostle made no distinction between those alive at the second coming of Christ and those who died beforehand. God will award the crown of righteousness "to *all* who have longed for his appearing." Clearly his counsel to "continue to live in [Christ], rooted and built up in him, strengthened in the faith as you were taught" (Col. 2:6, 7), holds the secret of a right standing with God for all believers alike to the end of time.

The teachings of Jesus reflect a similar concern. He counseled the disciples to be careful and watch in readiness so that the Second Advent would not take them by surprise. Our Saviour warned them against the false teachings and miracles that would "deceive even the elect—if that were possible" (Matt. 24:24). And He reminded them that only "he who stands firm to the end will be saved" (Matt. 10:22; cf. Mark 13:35, 36; Luke 21:34-36). Using the vine and the branches as an illustration, Jesus explained the need of abiding in Him, of remaining in His love (John 15:1-10). He seemed truly concerned about whether "the Son of Man . . . will . . . find *faith* on the earth" when He comes (Luke 18:8).

We therefore conclude: 1. According to the New Testament, all believers must have the merits of Christ for a right standing with God. Scripture focuses on the believer's faith relationship with the Saviour and stresses the absolute necessity to remain in Christ by faith until He returns. 2. Jesus and the apostolic writers give no indication that the last generation has to be special—that it has to succeed where all previous ones failed. Jesus and the apostles reveal no concern that believers may fail to climb high enough on the ladder of their character development and behavior modification. Instead, they concentrate on the danger that some may renounce their faith and break their spiritual union with Christ and in so doing lose access to the hope held out in the gospel.

Perhaps the most specific scriptural passage to describe the experience of the last generation of believers is the message to the church in Laodicea, recorded in Revelation 3:14-21. Adventists have always believed that it describes the last religious movement specifically singled out in Scripture, and that it therefore applies with particular force to us as a church. It is therefore proper that we should examine the message to establish whether it describes (1) a superior church able to stand on its own flawless morality and spiritual wholeness, or (2) a church fully dependent on Christ's redemptive role for a right standing with God, as we have seen earlier.

According to the testimony of "the faithful and true witness" (verse 14), the Laodiceans find themselves in a terrible predicament, being totally deceived about their true spiritual condition. 1. They think they are rich and in need of nothing, when in reality they are spiritually bankrupt. 2. They are guilty of the sins of self-righteousness and arrogance—sins contrary both to the law and to the gospel. 3. They live in a state of shameful spiritual nakedness, of pitifulness and blindness, of wretchedness and poverty. 4. They do not have either true faith or real love ("gold refined in the fire" (verse 18; cf. 1 Peter 1:7; Heb. 3:14; 11:7).

It is important to note that the Laodiceans' critical predicament is not a matter of sinful performance, but of sinful being. The fact that the Witness does not mention any specific sinful practices, such as idol worship, stealing, or adultery, suggests that they probably do not participate in many sinful behaviors practiced by those who do not care about God's moral standards. The Laodiceans have not openly rejected the law of God and, like the prodigal son, wasting their lives in sinful living. Instead, their condition is critical because they have not responded to the gospel in repentance and faith, and consequently they have no access to Christ's redemptive work.

According to the True Witness, the solution to the Laodiceans' almost desperate spiritual condition does not involve more and better works, nor is it an improved version of their own brand of garment—which is to say, of their personal righteousness, goodness, and merits. Instead, they can find the answer to their situation only in Christ and what He makes available to them. The Witness urges them to secure three specific things from Jesus (Rev. 3:18): (1) the "gold" of faith so that they may become rich by partaking of the abundance of Christ; (2) the "white clothes" of His saving righteousness to cover their shameful spiritual nakedness; and (3) the "salve" that will enable them to see their true spiritual condition, and move them to repent of their self-sufficiency so that God may forgive their sin and remove their guilt.

Christ also admonishes them to repent of their spiritual arrogance (see verse 19), and invites them to open the door to Him so He may have fellowship with them (verse 20). Those who heed the message and follow the urging of the Faithful Witness will be over-comers—they are the true believers who will sit with Jesus on His throne just as Jesus sat down with His Father on His throne (verse 21) after Jesus obtained His redemptive victory.

There is something rather peculiar—and really disturbing—about the format of the message to Laodicea. While the message is addressed to the church corporately, the final invitation and promise go, not to the church at large, but to individual persons within it. The last exhortation to the church as a church is an appeal to repentance (verse 19). The message then shifts from the corporate to the personal. Jesus says:

> I stand at the door and knock. If anyone hears my voice and opens the door, I will come in and eat with him, and he with me. To him who overcomes, I will give the right to sit with me on my throne, just as I overcame and sat down with my Father on his throne" (verses 20, 21).

The message to the Laodiceans suggests that this prophetic church faces the real danger of repeating the fatal mistake committed by so many in Israel at the time of Christ. As a corporate body, the Laodiceans apparently will never open the door to Christ as their only source of saving righteousness. They will probably continue in their religious pride, totally oblivious to their moral inadequacy and spiritual destitution. Apparently they will not answer the call of the gospel in repentance and faith. But if they do not, the True Witness will indeed spit them out of His mouth (verse 16). That is, God will have to reject them as a people, and they will lose their participation in God's covenant of grace. They will not be among the King's guests who will "eat" with Jesus (cf. verse 20 with Matt. 22:2-10).

Commenting on the message to Laodicea, Ellen White says:

> God calls for a spiritual revival and a spiritual reformation. Unless this takes place, those who are lukewarm will continue to grow more abhorrent to the Lord, until He will refuse to acknowledge them as His children (Selected Messages, book 1, p. 128).

But the message also suggests that Laodicea will include a remnant made up of those who heed the counsel and avail themselves of the provision Christ has made for them. They will overcome their spiritual self-sufficiency and open the door to Him. Recognizing their sinfulness, they will repent and be forgiven. They will cover their shameful spiritual nakedness with the white robe of Christ's perfect righteousness, and some day be part of the redeemed of all ages as guests at "the wedding of the Lamb" (Rev. 19:7).

John the revelator saw a vision of the "great multitude" of the redeemed "standing before the throne and before the Lamb, clothed in white robes" (Rev. 7:9, RSV). When the apostle inquired about their identity, he learned that they had "washed their robes and made them white in the blood of the Lamb. Therefore are they before the throne of God, and serve him day and night within his temple" (verses 14, 15, RSV). Clearly, the church victorious, the redeemed of all ages and of all peoples, are those who—to use the biblical metaphor—have washed their robes and made them white in the blood of Christ.

The expression *"therefore* are they before the throne of God . . ."* indicates that what has made it possible for them to live in God's holy presence, what has qualified them to serve Him in His temple, is the fact that they have been fully pardoned, that they are dressed in the garment of Christ's perfect righteousness. The last blessing of Scripture reinforces the importance of being washed clean in the blood of Christ. It reads: "Blessed are those who wash their robes, that they may have the right to the tree of life and may go through the gates into the city" (Rev. 22:14).

In one of his visions of heaven, John heard a great multitude shouting:

> Hallelujah! for our Lord God Almighty reigns. Let us rejoice and be glad and give him glory! For the wedding

of the Lamb has come, and his bride has made herself ready. Fine linen, bright and clean, was given her to wear (Rev. 19:6-8).

It is important to note that the bride—which is God's true church—did not develop, produce, or earn the "fine linen." This spiritual garment was *"given* her"—a telling illustration showing that the righteousness in which the redeemed will be arrayed they receive as a gift from God, thanks to their faith relationship with Christ.

We can recognize a close similarity between the experience and destiny of the church and that of Israel. As Israel was totally dependent on the typical ministry of the earthly priesthood, so the church is totally dependent on the mediatorial ministry of Christ in the presence of God in heaven (1 Tim. 2:5, 6; Heb. 7:25). The redeemed will eventually participate in the wedding feast of the Lamb and partake of the eternal inheritance, not because they achieved sinless perfection and thus outgrew their need of Christ's mediation, but because His mediatorial work was fully realized on their behalf the moment He secured for them God's final and irreversible verdict of acceptance at the pre-Advent judgment.

Such considerations lead us to at least the following conclusions: 1. The Scriptures do not support the idea that the last generation of believers will achieve a state of perfect spiritual righteousness and learn to live without sinning before the end of probation. 2. The last religious movement singled out in Scripture is as sinful, imperfect, and unworthy as any previous generation of believers, and consequently as dependent as all others on the imputed righteousness of Christ. 3. Only those in Laodicea who individually recognize their true spiritual condition, repent to secure God's forgiveness, and cover themselves in the white clothes of the saving righteousness of Christ will inherit eternal life. They are part of the "remnant chosen by grace" (Rom. 11:5) who will be living by faith when Jesus returns.

V   The Mediatorial Ministry of Christ Completed at the End of Probation

Christ's mediatorial ministry on behalf of those who approach the Father through Him will eventually end. At least three passages in Ellen White's writings state that during the "short time" between the end of probation and "the appearing of the Lord in the clouds of heaven" *(The Great Controversy,* p. 490), Jesus will not function as the mediator between God and man. Notice:

> Then there will be no Priest in the sanctuary to offer [the lost's] sacrifices, their confessions, and their prayers before the Father's throne *(Early Writings,* p. 48). Those who are living upon the earth when the intercession of Christ shall cease in the sanctuary above are to stand in the sight of a holy God without a mediator *(The Great Controversy,* p. 425). When [Jesus] leaves the sanctuary, darkness covers the inhabitants of the earth. In that fearful time the righteous must live in the sight of a holy God without an intercessor *(ibid.,* p. 614).

Having "to stand in the sight of a holy God without a mediator" can be a frightening prospect, particularly for those who have a man-centered conception of salvation—those who maintain that the believer on his own must achieve a righteousness of being and a flawlessness of conduct that will meet God's standard of perfection. However, when we understand what God does to make our salvation certain before Jesus lays down His high priestly robes, our fear turns into grateful joy for the marvelous plan God devised to make sure that none of those who trust in His grace for salvation will be disappointed. All who by faith avail themselves of Christ's redemptive work on their behalf will actually inherit eternal life.

We shall briefly discuss three basic reasons the believers can rest their cases with God in full assurance that He has devised a perfect plan to bring His people safely to the eternal kingdom. In view of that, they do not have to fear either the close of probation or the time of trouble that follows it.

First, Jesus will cease His mediatorial ministry only after the destiny of all the inhabitants of the earth has been permanently fixed and the salvation of His people is no longer in question.

> When the third angel's message closes, mercy no longer pleads for the guilty inhabitants of the earth. . . . An angel returning from the earth announces that his work is done; the final test has been brought upon the world, and all who have proved themselves loyal to the divine precepts have received "the seal of the living God." *Then Jesus ceases His intercession in the sanctuary above.* He lifts His hands and with a loud voice says, "It is done"; and all the angelic host lay off their crowns as He makes the solemn announcement: "He that is unjust, let him be unjust still: and he which is filthy, let him be filthy still: and he that is righteous, let him be righteous still: and he that is holy, let him be holy still" (Rev. 22:11). *Every case has been decided for life or death. Christ has made the atonement for His people and blotted out their sins. The number of His subjects is made up;* "the kingdom and dominion, and the greatness of the kingdom under the whole heaven," is about to be given to the heirs of salvation, and Jesus is to reign as King of kings and Lord of lords *(The Great Controversy,* pp. 613, 614; italics supplied).

When the work of the investigative judgment closes, the destiny of all will have been decided for life or death. Probation is ended a short time before the appearing of the Lord in the clouds of heaven *(ibid.,* p. 490). When *the irrevocable decision of the sanctuary has been pronounced and the destiny of the world has been forever fixed,* the inhabitants of the earth will know it not *(ibid.,* p. 615; italics supplied).

[Satan] sees that holy angels are guarding [God's people], and he infers that their sins have been pardoned; but he does not know that *their cases have been decided* in the sanctuary above *(ibid.,* p. 618; italics supplied). When Jesus ceases to plead for man, the cases of all are forever decided *(Testimonies,* vol. 2, p. 191).

Such statements highlight the fact that Jesus does not really just cease His mediatorial work, but rather that He completes it. Jesus does not stop functioning as man's representative with the Father without first making sure His ministry has achieved its intended purpose. He does not suddenly interrupt His work, leaving everyone standing on his own two feet, as it were. Instead, *Jesus finishes His mediation on behalf of His people by securing for them God's final and irreversible verdict of approval as the pre-Advent judgment comes to an end.* As a result, they receive "the seal of the living God," which grants their sonship in Christ a permanent status, and bestows upon them the right to be heirs of the kingdom.

Second, the moment when Jesus completes His mediation for the last generation of believers also marks the end of the pre-Advent judgment. The "final test" that determines eternal destinies "has been brought upon the world. . . . The number of His subjects is made up." As a result, the destiny of all is permanently and irrevocably fixed, each case not only decided but forever closed, never more to be opened for revision. Because the verdict God pronounces as the judgment comes to an end is final, those who will be saved are saved, and those who will be lost are lost *as of that moment*.

The reason that Jesus no longer mediates for His people after probation closes is that His mediation has already achieved its intended purpose, fully and completely. For one thing, God has declared the believers to be accepted as righteous in Christ. He has removed their guilt and forgiven their sin. Their names are permanently recorded in the Lamb's book of life and they are sealed for eternity. For another, the judgment has ended. The believers have passed the final test that decided their eternal destiny. The Mediator has answered Satan's arguments and accusations. The Judge has handed down His verdict, Jesus has won the case, and the trial is over—forever.

The third reason the believer does not need to be apprehensive about either the end of probation or the time of trouble is that God will provide special protection for His people during this period. Notice how the following statements bring this out:

> Jacob's history is also an assurance that God will not cast off those who have been deceived and tempted and betrayed into sin, but who have returned unto Him with true repentance. . . . God will send His angels to comfort and protect them in the time of peril. The assaults of Satan are fierce and determined, his delusions are terrible; but the Lord's eye is upon His people, and His ear listens to their cries. . . . God's love for His children during the period of their severest trial is as strong and tender as in the days of their sunniest prosperity (*The Great Controversy*, p. 621).

> Though enemies may thrust them into prison, yet dungeon walls cannot cut off the communication between their souls and Christ. One who sees their every weakness, who is acquainted with every trial, is above all earthly

powers; and angels will come to them in lonely cells, bringing light and peace from heaven. The prison will be as a palace; for the rich in faith dwell there, and the gloomy walls will be lighted up with heavenly light *(ibid.,* p. 627).

The people of God will not be free from suffering; but while persecuted and distressed, while they endure privation and suffer for want of food, they will not be left to perish. That God who cared for Elijah will not pass by one of His self-sacrificing children. He who numbers the hairs of their head will care for them, and in time of famine they shall be satisfied. While the wicked are dying from hunger and pestilence, angels will shield the righteous and supply their wants. . . . Could men see with heavenly vision, they would behold companies of angels that excel in strength stationed about those who have kept the word of Christ's patience. . . .

The heavenly sentinels, faithful to their trust, continue their watch. Though a general decree has fixed the time when commandment keepers may be put to death, their enemies will in some cases anticipate the decree, and before the time specified, will endeavor to take their lives. But none can pass the mighty guardians stationed about every faithful soul. Some are assailed in their flight from the cities and villages; but the swords raised against them break and fall powerless as a straw. Others are defended by angels in the form of men of war *(ibid.,* pp. 629-631).

At least three major factors will combine to give the believers peace, hope, and assurance: 1. Jesus will mediate in their behalf until God's final verdict of acceptance makes their eternal salvation secure. 2. They will not have to face an after-judgment test to determine whether or not they have achieved flawless righteousness of being and sinlessness of conduct and hence are personally worthy of eternal life. 3. God will protect and provide for them during the short period of time between the end of probation and the second coming of Christ, so that nothing will jeopardize their salvation.

The close of probation marks the end of the present order of things and introduces a totally different situation. As far as their eternal destiny is concerned, the inhabitants of the world have permanently been divided into two groups: those who are irremediably lost and those whose names stand permanently recorded in the Lamb's book of life. And each group will have a unique experience during the short time before Jesus' return.

Because the wicked have rejected God's final attempt to bring them to repentance, they now face the most undesirable conditions.

> Mercy no longer pleads for the guilty inhabitants of the earth. . . . The restraint which has been upon the wicked is removed, and Satan has entire control of the finally impenitent. God's long-suffering has ended. The world has rejected His mercy, despised His love, and trampled upon His law. The wicked have passed the boundary of their probation; the Spirit of God, persistently resisted, has been at last withdrawn. Unsheltered by divine grace, they have no protection from the wicked one. Satan will then plunge the inhabitants of the earth into one great, final trouble. As the angels of God cease to hold in check the fierce winds of human passion, all the elements of strife will be let loose. The whole world will be involved in ruin more terrible than that which came upon Jerusalem of old (*ibid.*, pp. 613, 614).

We can describe the experience of "the finally impenitent" as follows: 1. The Holy Spirit, removed from them, no longer motivates them to repentance and faith in Christ—which means that there no longer exists any possibility that they can be reconciled to God. 2. God leaves them entirely under the unrestricted control of

Satan. 3. They go through a time of extreme trouble, strife, and ruin. 4. And they receive God's judgment in the form of the seven last plagues *(ibid.,* pp. 627-629).

What happens to God's people during the time of trouble is almost the exact opposite of what happens to the wicked, and falls into two separate yet interrelated parts. First, as the wicked live under the total power of Satan, so the redeemed dwell under the supernatural protection and leading of God. We have already seen that through angels and other providences God will shield them from life-threatening danger and want. The following passage indicates that God will also shelter them from any experience that does not contribute to the accomplishment of His specific purpose for them during this time.

> The eye of God, looking down the ages, was fixed upon the crisis which His people are to meet, when earthly powers shall be arrayed against them. Like the captive exile, they will be in fear of death by starvation or by violence. But the Holy One who divided the Red Sea before Israel will manifest His mighty power and turn their captivity. "They shall be mine, saith the Lord of hosts, in that day when I make up my jewels; and I will spare them, as a man spareth his own son that serveth him" (Mal. 3:17). If the blood of Christ's faithful witnesses were shed at this time, it would not, like the blood of the martyrs, be as seed sown to yield a harvest for God. Their fidelity would not be a testimony to convince others of the truth; for the obdurate heart has beaten back the waves of mercy until they return no more. If the righteous were now left to fall a prey to their enemies, it would be a triumph for the prince of darkness. Says the psalmist: "In the time of trouble he shall hide me in his pavilion: in the secret of his tabernacle shall he hide me" (Ps. 27:5). Christ has spoken: "Come, my people, enter thou into thy chambers, and shut thy doors about thee: hide thyself as

it were for a little moment, until the indignation be overpast. For, behold, the Lord cometh out of his place to punish the inhabitants of the earth for their iniquity" (Isa. 26:20, 21). Glorious will be the deliverance of those who have patiently waited for His coming and whose names are written in the book of life *(ibid.,* p. 634).

Since the judgment is finished and human probation is ended, it would be purposeless to expose God's people to needless trials, temptations, and danger. After all, their cases have been decided, their destiny established. They are God's people—His precious jewels—with their names permanently written in the Lamb's book of life. So it is logical that God should carefully monitor their experience during this time—that He should control Satan's reach and bid them to hide "as it were for a little moment, until the indignation be overpast," and "spare them, as a man spareth his own son."

This reinforces something we have seen earlier, namely that the destiny of God's people is forever established at that moment when the world's probation closes and the pre-Advent judgment finishes. At that time God forever removes their "filthy garments."

> The spotless robe of Christ's righteousness is placed upon the tried, tempted, yet faithful children of God. The despised remnant are clothed in glorious apparel, *never-more to be defiled by the corruptions of the world.* Their names are retained in the Lamb's book of life, enrolled among the faithful of all ages *(Testimonies,* vol. 5, p. 475; italics supplied).

The second aspect of the experience God's people have during the time of trouble is one of deep spiritual intensity, of sincere self-examination and of earnest wrestling with God. Satan will do his best "to terrify them with the thought that their cases are hopeless, that the stain of their defilement will never be washed away," and attempt "to destroy their faith" in God *(The Great Controversy,* p. 619). Ellen White compares their experience to the night Jacob struggled with the Angel before he met his angry brother, Esau, after many years of separation:

> Jacob's night of anguish, when he wrestled in prayer for deliverance from the hand of Esau (Gen. 32:24-30), represents the experience of God's people in the time of trouble *(ibid.,* p. 616).

Obviously Jacob's experience during his "night of anguish" only symbolizes what God's people will experience during the time of trouble, and therefore no one should attempt to establish a direct and complete correlation between the two. We must respect both the similarities *and* the differences. Among the similarities that bear most directly on our present study are: (1) the spiritual condition of the subjects involved, (2) the test to which they are subjected, and (3) the victory they win. We shall briefly examine each.

1. The Spiritual Condition of God's People During the Time of Trouble

Jacob was personally acquainted with the God of his fathers and knew that the Lord had chosen him to be a direct heir to the covenant promises He had made to his grandfather Abraham. Throughout Jacob's life God had protected, guided, and blessed him in rather unusual ways. Yet when Jacob faced that night of agony, he was a "sinful, erring mortal" who confessed "his weakness and unworthiness" *(ibid.,* p. 617), who experienced "the crushing weight of self-reproach, for it was his own sin that had brought this danger," and who, consequently, knew that "his only hope was in the mercy of God" *(ibid.,* p. 616).

112

END OF PROBATION

In this sense God's people after the end of probation are no different from Jacob. Living at such a decisive time in the world's history, when they can so clearly perceive the Lord's hand in human affairs, gives them a unique experience with God. But they are far from being sinlessly perfect. The record of their lives is such that "as they review the past, their hopes sink; for in their whole lives they can see little good. They are fully conscious of their weakness and unworthiness" (*ibid.*, pp. 618, 619). Though surrounded by enemies, their greatest concern is not their physical danger but that they have repented and received God's pardon for all their sins. They have "a keen sense of self-reproach" that they didn't do more for Christ in the past so that now they might have "more power to resist and urge back the mighty tide of evil" (*ibid.*, p. 619).

According to Ellen White, God's people are "placed in the furnace of fire" during the time of trouble because "their earthliness must be consumed, that the image of Christ may be perfectly reflected" (*ibid.*, p. 621). Since this happens after the pre-Advent judgment, we see clearly that God's people do not achieve a state of sinless perfection by the time probation ends and the time of trouble begins. It further shows that God seals their eternal destiny in spite of the fact that "earthliness" still lingers in their lives and consequently the image of Christ is not yet "perfectly reflected" in them.

Obviously, then, the believers who live through the time of trouble are not a generation of supersaints who have fully attained a state of total sanctification of being. Like Jacob, they are imperfect and unworthy and, save for God's grace as manifested in Christ's redemptive mediation on their behalf, have no righteousness of their own on which to claim eternal life.

As is the case with all previous generations of believers, God's remnant church will be made perfect only at the second coming of Christ. Through the resurrection/glorification event, God will restore His people to the original state of spiritual wholeness Adam and Eve enjoyed before the Fall. As a result, all the redeemed sinners will then, for the first time ever, reflect the Redeemer's image as fully as our first parents exhibited the Creator's image in their primal state. In the meantime the people of God can be perfectly righteous, holy, and worthy only in Christ.

2. The Nature of the Test God's People Have to Endure During the Time of Trouble

We have here one of those instances when one can better understand what something is by first establishing what it is not. So let us begin by briefly describing two kinds of tests that, although similar in form, have a different purpose and outcome. The first test determines whether someone qualifies for an intended purpose. It creates a pass-or-fail situation. If the candidate performs as expected, he passes; but if his performance is below the established standard, he is disqualified.

The second type of test improves, strengthens, or polishes the capabilities of someone who has already been tested and accepted as adequate. The pass-fail element is absent here. For example, before an Olympic team chooses a particular athlete as a member, he must make it through some rigorous qualifying tests. Whether or not he becomes a regular member of this select group depends on his performance. Once he is selected, he engages in a variety of exercises, practices, and competitions. Each is a test in its own right. But their purpose is to improve his performance, not to decide whether or not he will officially participate in the

Olympic games. That decision rests on previous testing and does not change now.

The test Jacob encountered during his night of trial and the one God's people will endure during the time of trouble belong to the second category. The test God's people will endure will not decide whether or not they will be participants of His redemptive covenant. That decision has already been made. Instead, God has designed their test as a means to achieve three basic objectives: (1) to destroy all remaining confidence in their own ability to deliver themselves; (2) to lead them to a full realization of their unworthiness to be heirs of God's covenant blessings—they must be fully persuaded that they are saved by grace alone; and (3) to strengthen their faith in and dependence on the mercy of God for the fulfillment of His covenant promises.

Let us examine Jacob's case first. God had appointed him as the heir of His covenant with Abraham even before Jacob's birth (see Gen. 25:23). On the night of his trial Jacob already had both Isaac's birthright blessing and God's confirmation of the covenant (Gen. 27:17-29; 28:10-15), in spite of the fact that he was an imperfect and unworthy sinner. So Jacob's experience that night was not intended to determine whether he was worthy of the covenant promises. God had obviously made that decision long ago. Instead, the test examined the patriarch's faith: faith that God had forgiven his sins and that in His mercy He would deliver him from the impending danger and fulfill His covenant promises to him.

> Having sent his family away, that they may not witness his distress, Jacob remains alone to intercede with God. He confesses his sin and gratefully acknowledges the mercy of God toward him while with deep humiliation he pleads the covenant made with his fathers and the prom-

ises to himself in the night vision at Bethel and in the land of his exile. . . . Long has he endured perplexity, remorse, and trouble for his sin; now he must have the assurance that it is pardoned. . . .

Satan had accused Jacob before the angels of God, claiming the right to destroy him because of his sin; he . . . endeavored to force upon him a sense of his guilt in order to discourage him and break his hold upon God (*ibid.*, pp. 616-618).

Jacob recognized his inability to deliver himself from the impending danger. He admitted his sinfulness, imperfection, and unworthiness to be an heir to the covenant promises. Yet he did not yield to Satan's attempts to have him abandon his faith in God. That is why he based his hope of deliverance, not on his personal merits—for he had none—but on "the mercy of a covenant-keeping God" (*ibid.*, p. 617).

The experience of God's people as they go through the time of trouble is similar to Jacob's in this regard. We have previously seen that God's final and irreversible verdict at the pre-Advent judgment has already fixed their eternal destiny. God in Christ has already appointed them as heirs of the kingdom. Their names stand permanently recorded in the Lamb's book of life, not because they are righteous and worthy, but because they accepted the salvation God provided in Christ. And yet they go through a time of intense trial. Notice:

As Satan accuses the people of God on account of their sins, the Lord permits him to try them to the uttermost. *Their confidence in God, their faith and firmness, will be severely tested.* As they review the past, their hopes sink; for in their whole lives they can see little good. They are fully conscious of their weakness and unworthiness. Satan endeavors to terrify them with the thought that their cases are hopeless, that the stain of their defilement will never be washed away. He hopes so to destroy their faith that they will yield to his temptations and turn from their allegiance to God. . . . They afflict their souls before God, pointing to their past repentance of their many sins. . . . Their faith does not fail. . . .

If the people of God had unconfessed sins to appear before them while tortured with fear and anguish, they would be overwhelmed; despair would cut off their faith, and they could not have confidence to plead with God for deliverance. But while they have a deep sense of their unworthiness, they have no concealed wrongs to reveal. Their sins have gone beforehand to judgment and have been blotted out, and they cannot bring them to remembrance. . . . The season of distress and anguish before us will require a faith that can endure weariness, delay, and hunger—a faith that will not faint though severely tried (*ibid.*, pp. 618-621; italics supplied).

Clearly, the trying experience God's people will have after He permanently establishes their eternal destiny is not designed to determine whether they will be saved or not. Nor is it meant to find out whether or not they have developed spotless righteousness of being. Instead, it reveals that they recognize their helplessness and unworthiness, that they have confessed their guilt and depend on God's forgiveness for absolution, and that they do not yield to Satan's attempts to destroy their faith in God for deliverance.

3. The Victory God's People Win During the Time of Trouble

Another comparison Ellen White establishes between Jacob's night of anguish and the experience of God's people during the time of trouble is the victory they win—how they obtain deliverance from the immediate danger and continue enjoying their covenant relationship with God.

> [Jacob's] was the assurance of one who confesses his weakness and unworthiness, yet trusts the mercy of a covenant-keeping God. "He had power over the angel, and prevailed" (Hosea 12:4). Through humiliation, repentance, and self-surrender, this sinful, erring mortal prevailed with the Majesty of heaven. He had fastened his trembling grasp upon the promises of God, and the heart of Infinite Love could not turn away the sinner's plea. As an evidence of his triumph and an encouragement to others to imitate his example, his name was changed from one which was a reminder of his sin, to one that commemorated his victory. . . . He had sincerely repented of his great sin, and he appealed to the mercy of God. He would not be turned from his purpose, but held fast the Angel and urged his petition with earnest, agonizing cries until he prevailed (*ibid.*, pp. 617, 618).

Jacob's triumph had obviously little to do with either spiritual accomplishments, moral development, righteous character, or sinless behavior. His great accomplishment that night was that he "prevailed with the Majesty of heaven," and not that he transcended his fallen condition and attained to a state of flawless perfection. His victory was, in essence, the assurance that God would deliver him from immediate danger and retain him as an heir of His gracious covenant, in spite of his unworthiness for such a special privilege.

His victory is also the secret of the victory for God's people during the time of trouble.

> Jacob's history is also an assurance that God will not cast off those who have been deceived and tempted and betrayed into sin, but who have returned unto Him with true repentance. . . . Jacob prevailed because he was persevering and determined. His victory is an evidence of

the power of importunate prayer. All who will lay hold of God's promises, as he did, and be as earnest and persevering as he was, will succeed as he succeeded *(ibid.,* p. 621). As they endeavor to wait trustingly for the Lord to work they are led to exercise faith, hope, and patience, which have been too little exercised during their religious experience. . . . The time of trouble is a fearful ordeal for God's people; but it is the time for every true believer to look up, and by faith he may see the bow of promise encircling him *(ibid.,* pp. 631-633).

We can attribute the triumph of Jacob on his night of anguish and the victory of God's people during the time of trouble to three separate yet complementary factors: (1) open acknowledgement of their unworthiness to participate in the covenant blessings; (2) sincere repentance for their sins and pleading for the assurance of God's forgiveness; (3) unyielding faith that in His mercy God will deliver them from present danger and fulfill the promises of the covenant, in spite of their obvious shortcomings, imperfection, and sinfulness.

The believers of the last generation will recognize that "it is through the grace of our Lord Jesus that [they] are saved," just as everyone else (Acts 15:11). They will gladly admit:

> He saved us, not because of righteous things we had done, but because of his mercy. He saved us through the washing of rebirth and renewal by the Holy Spirit . . . so that, having been justified by his grace, we might become heirs having the hope of eternal life (Titus 3:5-7).

The prevailing mood of all the redeemed will be one of gratitude and praise to God precisely because they are equally aware that it was His grace, as expressed in the redemption He provided in Christ, that made eternal life a reality for them. That is why they will forever be mindful of the fact that their presence in

God's eternal kingdom is, not an evidence of their personal righteousness, works, or merits, but a telling demonstration of the everlasting love, the infinite grace, and the unwavering faithfulness of the covenant-keeping God.

4. Some Scriptural Considerations

The classic text for an idea of the end of probation reads:

> He that is unjust, let him be unjust still: and he which is filthy, let him be filthy still: and he that is righteous, let him be righteous still: and he that is holy, let him be holy still (Rev. 22:11, KJV).

Scripture does not provide any details concerning either the specific historical moment of the verdict or the conditions that will prevail between the time of God's pronouncement and the second coming of Christ. All that we can say with reasonable certainty is that (1) it is a divine, final, and irreversible verdict that (2) divides mankind into two separate groups and (3) fixes everybody's eternal destiny forever. Since God's judgment permanently seals the unjust in their unjust state and the righteous in their righteous state, it logically follows that no one will change sides afterward. A decision has been made concerning who belongs where, and it stands unchanged.

The concept of the end of probation and the fixation of destinies also appears in some of Christ's parables, particularly that of the 10 virgins. This parable contains at least three details relevant to our present discussion. First, the virgins divide into those who go in with the bridegroom "to the wedding banquet" (Matt. 25:10) and those not prepared to do so. Second, those who do not enter with the bridegroom cannot join the wedding party later—they lose forever their opportunity to take part in the wedding.

Third, when after their unsuccessful search for oil the foolish ones return, the bridegroom denies them entrance into the wedding hall, saying, "I tell you the truth, I don't know you" (verse 12). Clearly, the reason for their rejection is their lack of a personal acquaintance with the bridegroom. In theological terms we would probably say that they do not have a close faith relationship with Jesus Christ as their personal Saviour. They probably have other fine qualifications, but because they are strangers to Christ, they have no access to the wedding.

According to the parable, all 10 young ladies had lamps, representing "the word of God," but the foolish ones had no reserve of oil, "a symbol of the Holy Spirit" (*Christ's Object Lessons,* pp. 406, 407). In a theological sense we should not construe this to mean either that God arbitrarily withheld the Spirit from them or that they somehow were unable to retain Him. Previously we saw that our faith relationship with Christ gives us access to the blessings of the covenant of grace—He is "the medium through which Heaven's blessings" come to His people (*The Desire of Ages,* p. 357). And since the sealing of the Spirit is one of those blessings, it follows that only those who live in a faith relationship with Christ can have the Spirit in this particular sense. Consequently we see that while their lack of oil was a perceptible *evidence* of their unreadiness, the real *cause* of their problem was the absence of a personal faith connection to the Saviour.

A personal relationship with Jesus Christ as the basic factor in a person's eternal destiny is illustrated elsewhere in the Gospels, as well. In Matthew 7, Jesus predicted that at the judgment many will come to Him, saying:

> "Lord, Lord, did we not prophesy in your name, and cast out demons in your name, and do many mighty works in your name?" And then will I declare to them, "I never knew you; depart from me, you evildoers" (verses 22, 23, RSV).

To prophesy, expel demons, and do mighty deeds in Christ's name are definitely good works. Unfortunately such things do not reconcile a sinner with God—they are incapable of granting him adoption into God's spiritual family or giving him access to His eternal inheritance. So the problem of the people in Matthew 7:22 is that they have a behavior-centered conception of salvation. Instead of relying on Christ's redemptive work on their behalf, they expect to be welcomed into the kingdom on the basis of the things they did in Christ's name.

Christ's declaration to them reveals two significant facts: 1. Only those Jesus personally knows—those He has engraved in the palms of His hands because they accepted His redemptive work on their behalf—will enter the kingdom of glory. All others will remain outside regardless of what they may have done or the qualifications they may possess. 2. Good works—even such outstanding things as prophesying and exorcising demons, things that require superior spiritual powers—cannot do for man what God has determined only a personal faith relationship with Christ will accomplish. As a result, those who come presenting to God their own "mighty works" rather than Christ's redemptive work imputed to them by faith He counts as "evildoers."

Christ's faithfulness in finishing His work on the cross guarantees that He will finish His work on the throne. As Jesus hung on Calvary's cross, the bystanders mocked and humiliated Him, urging Him to save Himself from such a horrible death. The rulers, the common people, the Roman soldiers, and even one of the crucified criminals challenged Him to prove His Messiahship by coming down from the cross (Luke 23:35-39). But no person or thing could persuade Jesus to leave the cross until He had fully accomplished the purpose of His earthly mission. He must give His life as the atoning sacrifice to reconcile humanity to God. We can therefore rest assured that He will not leave the heavenly throne or cease His mediation on our behalf until He finishes applying the benefits of His redemptive work to secure the salvation of those He purchased with His blood.

The fact that Jesus took the penalty for our sin upon Himself assures us that He will face God's judgment as our representative. The judgment is real, and it has eternal consequences. But thanks to Jesus, it is not a time of wrath for the believer. For him the cup of God's unmitigated judgment on sin has already been poured out—it is empty. The Saviour drank every last drop of it so that those who accept His redemptive activity on their behalf will never have to taste the eternal consequences of sin. "Their sins have gone beforehand to judgment and have been blotted out" (*The Great Controversy,* p. 620). As a result, they stand blameless in Christ before God.

While it is true that Jesus will not act as our mediator during the time of trouble, we can rest assured that He will not leave us alone. Jesus promised never to forsake us, but will be with us "always, to the very end of the age" (Matt. 28:20; see Heb. 13:5). We can therefore rest secure in the faithfulness of God, who is both willing and able to keep His own. After all, Jesus said:

> My sheep listen to my voice; I know them, and they follow me. I give them eternal life, and they shall never perish. . . . My Father, who has given them to me, is greater than all; no one can snatch them out of my Father's hand (John 10:27-29).

VI Ellen G. White and a Deception Aimed Particularly at Adventists

Adventists believe that a major aspect of "our" message is to lift up Jesus before the world as the living Saviour who is personally completing man's redemption in the presence of the Father today. The irony is that, as the history of the movement shows, some Adventists have always found it difficult to keep their eyes fixed, and their assurance of salvation based, on Christ's mediatorial ministry in heaven. They have been more concerned about their own accomplishments—their character development and behavior modification—than about their faith participation in the atoning death, redemptive victory, and all-sufficient righteousness of Christ.

According to Ellen White, one of the greatest deceptions the church contended with in the past will make its inroads into Adventism again in the future (see *Selected Messages,* book 2, p. 36). It is an error that places undue emphasis on—and has unrealistic expectations of—what the believer supposedly can accomplish in his present life with the help of the Spirit. Because of its one-sided emphasis, such "fanaticism" fails to attribute the right value both to the redemptive work Christ finished as the atoning sacrifice on the cross and to the mediatorial work He is presently carrying on as man's representative-advocate with the Father on the throne.

We can divide Ellen White's writings on this subject into three general parts: (1) what happened shortly after the 1844 disappointment, (2) what happened at the turn of the century, and (3) what she believed will happen again shortly before the return of Christ.

1. What Happened Shortly After the 1844 Disappointment

Ellen White reports that "in the period of disappointment after the passing of the time in 1844, fanaticism in various forms arose" (ibid., p. 34). The worst of them had three basic elements: First, some Adventists believed in total sanctification of being. "They declared that they were perfected, that body, soul, and spirit were holy" (ibid.). Second, they concluded that they could live without sinning. They "claimed that they were sanctified, that they could not sin" (ibid., p. 27).

This second point we can understand in at least two ways: 1. Since their sanctification of being had been completed, they were now able to live in total harmony with God's entire will for humanity—they could obey the law flawlessly, and therefore were no longer dependent on the imputed righteousness of Christ for their standing with Him. 2. Because they were holy, whatever they did was right. Having transcended both their sinful natures and the requirements of the law, they were beyond the moral principles and ethical standards that regulated the lives of those who had not reached their level of supposed spiritual development.

Third, they taught that the attainment of such complete inner sanctification and total outward compliance with God's will was a requirement for salvation to those living at the time of the Second Advent. Those listening to their views "were pressed beyond measure to receive the message of error; it was represented to them that unless they did this they would be lost" (ibid., pp. 34, 35).

One of the greatest negative consequences of this deception was its disruption of the believer's faith relationship with Jesus Christ as the only way for a right standing with God, and the only source of saving righteousness. Notice:

> We must have a knowledge of ourselves, a knowledge that will result in contrition, before we can find pardon and peace. . . . *It is only he who knows himself to be a sinner that Christ can save (Christ's Object Lessons,* p. 158; italics supplied). Our love to Christ will be in proportion to the depth of our conviction of sin *(Faith and Works,* p. 96). Apart from Christ we have no merit, no righteousness *(Selected Messages,* book 1, p. 333). When men see their own nothingness, they are prepared to be clothed with the righteousness of Christ *(The Faith I Live By,* p. 111). Righteousness without a blemish can be obtained only through the imputed righteousness of Christ (Ellen G. White, in *Review and Herald,* Sept. 3, 1901).

As long as the believer recognizes himself to be a fallen, imperfect, and unworthy sinner, he will focus his attention and base his hope of salvation on his participation in the righteousness of Christ. He will continue looking to Jesus as "the author and perfecter of [his] faith" (Heb. 12:2). However, when he assumes that he can satisfy God's standard of righteousness in his own life by achieving holiness of being and sinlessness of conduct, then he mistakenly makes his personal accomplishments, instead of Christ's merits, the ultimate basis of his acceptance with God. As a result, he rejects Christ as the only way for a fallen being to secure salvation and eternal life.

2. What Happened at the Turn of the Century

Judging by articles he wrote, Elder E. R. Jones's understanding of true conversion included at least the following two major aspects: First, "complete transformation of vile man into the image of Jesus Christ" *(Review and Herald,* July 9, 1889). That is, he believed that the truly converted person will transcend or totally neutralize his sinful nature—he achieves a state of complete sanctification—so that instead of being "vile" as before, he now reflects the image of Christ fully in his own person.

Second, "complete cleansing from the power that compelled us to transgress" the law of God *(ibid.,* Mar. 12, 1889). The idea is that since the power that used to move him to sin is now cleansed, the truly converted believer no longer has sinful inclinations or evil desires. As a result, he can now live without sinning. Notice that Jones used the word *complete* with reference to both the inner transformation of being and the outward change in conduct.

After quoting 2 Corinthians 5:21, Jones stated: "To be made the righteousness of God in Him is to be made right as Christ is right; 'and *in* Him is no sin' (1 John 3:5, KJV)" *(ibid.,* July 9, 1889). Notice the subtle yet significant change that has taken place here. Paul is saying that God makes us righteous through Christ—we are righteous *in Christ.* That is, we participate in Christ's righteousness by faith, and are accounted righteous by virtue of the fact that His merits are imputed to us. The following passage expresses Paul's concept clearly:

> The only way in which [the sinner] can attain to righteousness is through faith. By faith he can bring to God the merits of Christ. . . . Christ's righteousness is accepted in place of man's failure, and God . . . treats him as though he were righteous, and loves him as He loves His Son. *This is how faith is accounted righteousness (Selected Messages,* book 1, p. 367; italics supplied).

DECEPTION AIMED

Elder Jones, on the other hand, was suggesting something radically different. He believed that we are "made right *as Christ is right.*" Since "in him is no sin," it follows that we must have no sin in us either—we must be sinless, just like Jesus. The implication is that we must become righteous in ourselves as Jesus was in Himself. We must develop a righteousness that measures up to the perfect righteousness of Christ in all respects—a righteousness on the basis of which we can stand fault-less before God.

Jones's articles contain hardly any reference to Christ as our representative on the cross to remove our guilt and cancel our death sentence. Nor do they say much about His mediatorial work in heaven, where He presently applies His atoning death, His redemptive victory, and His saving righteousness to those who accept Him as their personal Saviour. Jones concentrated exclusively on what the believer himself experiences in his present life.

His view represents a radical departure from the biblical gospel in at least three significant ways: First, it introduces a change in Christ's role as the Saviour of the world. While in theory he recognized Jesus as Saviour—particularly in the sense that He initially reconciles us to God—in practice he reduced Him to being an objective standard of holiness we must achieve, a model whose perfection we must duplicate in our personal lives, following the exact method that made victory possible for Him. As a result, *Christ's role changes from that of One who saves lost sinners through His redemptive work on their behalf to that of One who simply shows lost sinners how to save themselves by becoming as righteous, holy, and sinless as He is.*

Second, Jones's view minimizes the significance of Christ's role as mediator between God and man. At best, it reduces His mediatorial role to that of granting the believers forgiveness for past sins and supplying them with divine power to enable them to overcome sin and develop perfect righteousness in their own personal lives. At worst, Jones's theology bypasses or neutralizes the mediatorial ministry of Christ altogether. He introduces a method by which the believer can be as righteous—and consequently as worthy—as Jesus Himself.

Because Jesus was totally sinless, righteous, and holy, He needed no one to mediate between Him and the Father. He lived in direct and unhindered spiritual union with the other two Persons of the Godhead. Therefore, if the believer is indeed able to become sinlessly perfect like Christ—as Jones claimed—then it logically follows that whenever he reaches that goal, he also outgrows his need of Jesus as his personal advocate with the Father. Because he now is as righteous as Christ, he no longer needs a mediator to intercede on his behalf and keep him in a right relationship with God.

Third, Jones's view causes the believer to shift the focus of his attention and the basis of his assurance from Christ and His redemptive work to his own character development and behavior modification. Paul's example indicates that in order to be right with God the believer must surrender what he is, what he has, and what he does so that he may gain Christ (see Phil. 3:7, 8). Only then will he not have a righteousness of his own, but the righteousness of Christ "that comes from God and is by faith" (verse 9). In contrast, Jones's view encourages the believer to keep what he has, work on it until it is as good as what Christ has to offer, and then literally secure God's final verdict of approval on the basis of the righteousness he developed in his own life.

About a year after the publication of his articles, Ellen White wrote Elder Jones a lengthy and rather pointed letter. In it she cautioned him about his unbalanced mind, rebuked him for his improper use of both the Scriptures and her writings, and pointed out his extreme ideas. Among other things, she stated:

> It is not essential for you to know and tell others all the whys and wherefores as to what constitutes the new heart, or as to the position they can and must reach so as never to sin. You have no such work to do. . . . You will take passages in the Testimonies that speak of the close of probation, of the shaking among God's people, and you will talk of a coming out from this people of a purer, holier people that will arise *(Selected Messages,* book 1, pp. 177-179).

When we combine Elder Jones's assertions and this statement from Ellen White's writings, a clear scenario begins to emerge. *Jones was teaching that before the close of probation God's people can and must develop a personal righteousness that is as radical and complete—and consequently as meritorious—as that of Christ.* In other words, they must be as pure, sinless, and holy as Christ was and learn to live without sinning, as He lived.

Ellen White did not endorse his teachings. On the contrary, she called them "extreme ideas," and advised him not to take a course that would "create dissension" *(ibid.,* p. 179). Notice the following warning she gave Jones:

> Should many accept the views you advance, and talk and act upon them, we would see one of the greatest fanatical excitements that has ever been witnessed among Seventh-day Adventists. This is what Satan wants *(ibid.).*

Ten years after Ellen White penned this warning— or was it a prediction?—it became true. The so-called holy flesh doctrine became prevalent in Indiana. And, according to her own account, it had all the ingredients of the fanaticism she had met and condemned before (*ibid.*, book 2, pp. 33, 34), namely the desire (1) to achieve *total sanctification of being*—to outgrow or completely neutralize one's sinful nature and develop flawless righteousness in one's own person; (2) *to have the ability to live in perfect harmony with all the requirements of the law*—to learn to live without sinning; and (3) *to make the attainment of this superior level of spiritual development and moral behavior a requirement for those who will be alive when Jesus comes.*

According to this view, those who do not achieve such a sinless state can still be saved, but they will die first (see R. W. Schwarz, *Light Bearers to the Remnant* [Mountain View, Calif.: Pacific Press Pub. Assn., 1979], p. 447). The concept teaches that God requires a higher degree of righteousness of those who will be alive at the second coming of Christ than of all previous generations of believers. Those who will die before the end of probation can be righteous by faith in Christ in spite of the fact that they are still sinful, imperfect, and unworthy in themselves. They can avail themselves of God's forgiveness to make up for their faulty behavior, and of Christ's imputed righteousness to compensate for their imperfection of being. In contrast, those alive when Jesus returns must reach a state of sinless perfection. The righteousness of both their character and their conduct must be total, complete. In fact, they must be just as flawless, holy, and worthy as Jesus Himself.

Those who support such a view argue basically as follows: First, while Christ mediates for His people, the believers have access to both God's forgiveness and Christ's imputed righteousness to cover their sin and make up for their personal shortcomings. During this time God ultimately decides their destiny on the basis of whether or not they avail themselves of His provision mediated through Christ. God grants them eternal life on the basis that they were made blameless, holy, and worthy through the Saviour's merits imputed to them by faith.

Second, once probation closes and Christ's mediation ends, the believers' eternal destiny becomes totally dependent upon the perfection of their own righteousness and the flawlessness of their personal conduct. If they have a complete righteousness of being and have learned to live without sinning—just like Jesus—then they will inherit eternal life. However, should their personal righteousness somehow fail to measure up to God's standard of perfection, or should they so much as entertain a single evil thought during this time, they would be irremediably lost.

From this we can see that, according to this view, humanity has only two ways to be sure of eternal life: (1) to die while Jesus is still mediating before the Father, or (2) to achieve complete spiritual wholeness and learn to live in absolute obedience to God's total will for man before the world's probation comes to an end.

The first part of this argument is in full harmony with Scripture and consistent with what we have seen earlier in Ellen White's writings. However, when we examine the dynamics created by the second part of this view, we soon realize that it not only departs radically from the biblical gospel but also contradicts the scenario portrayed in Ellen White's writings. It is therefore not surprising that this "fanaticism," this "message of error," as Ellen White calls it, had some definitely negative results. Notice:

> These things bring a reproach upon the cause of truth, and hinder the proclamation of the last message of mercy to the world. . . . Those who have entered into and sustained this fanaticism might far better be engaged in

secular labor; for by their inconsistent course of action they are dishonoring the Lord and imperiling His people.
. . .

By this, unbelievers are led to think that Seventh-day Adventists are a set of fanatics. Thus prejudice is created that prevents souls from receiving the message for this time *(Selected Messages,* book 2, pp. 35, 36).

It was represented to them [certain people] that unless they did this [reached a state of total sanctification of being and sinlessness of behavior] they would be lost; and as the result their mind was unbalanced, and some became insane *(ibid.,* pp. 34, 35).

We will touch on five points brought out in her statements: 1. Such teachings do not constitute the message God has for the world at this time—they are not something Adventists are to believe and teach. 2. Instead, these teachings bring reproach upon Adventism and hinder the final proclamation of mercy to the world. 3. God's last message for the world—the one He invites Adventists to accept, believe, and proclaim—is a *"message of mercy,"* with all that such an expression implies.

4. Those who entered into and sustained the fanaticism dishonored the Lord and imperiled His people. The fanatics were not fit to teach religious subjects and would have been much better off in secular labor. 5. The fanaticism created such psychological pressure on some people that they lost their reason and became insane.

Many of the meetings that presented these extreme ideas exhibited a high pitch of emotionalism. People shouted, played music, even indulged in some forms of dancing. Speaking of such activities, Ellen White wrote:

This is an invention of Satan to cover up his ingenious methods for making of none effect the pure, sincere, elevating, ennobling, sanctifying truth for this time *(ibid., p. 36)*.

It is important that we distinguish between what constitutes the deception itself and what was merely part of the atmosphere created to predispose people to accept it. The high level of emotionalism, the music, the shouting, and other such practices that Ellen White called "a bedlam of noise" *(ibid.)* were not the theological distortion itself. They were "an invention of Satan *to cover up*" the real aberration. The deception itself was theological and had to do with three points already discussed earlier in this chapter: being flawlessly righteous, living without sinning, and attaining this state shortly before Christ comes.

Ellen White's reaction to such teachings leaves no question as to where she stood. First, she labeled them an error, a fallacy, fanaticism, fanciful and forbidden schemes, man-made tests, a delusion, an infatuation, an invention of Satan. Such are but some of the terms she used in her testimonies against them. Second, she expressed her own understanding of the issue enough to show that it disagrees with all three of the points advocated by the holy flesh people *(ibid., pp. 32-35)*.

Many Adventists are aware that a similar deception appeared again in the late 1950s. For more than a decade Robert Brinsmead and his followers advocated ideas that closely resembled those we have been considering. Schwarz rightly states that "Brinsmead's beliefs were an intellectual counterpart to the holy flesh movement of 60 years earlier" *(Light Bearers to the Remnant, p. 458)*. And, as did their predecessors, Brinsmead and his brother "felt compelled to make them [their extreme views] normative for the entire church" *(ibid.)*. With a dedication and a zeal worthy of a better cause, they spared no effort in their aggressive campaign to persuade the entire Adventist community that theirs was the only right position and that all other views were a departure from traditional Adventism.

In summary, the teaching Ellen White so decidedly opposed as a message of error has three major parts: The first one refers to the believer's person, his being or character—*who he is*. The claim is made that he must become sinless in character. In fact, he achieves a state of holiness and develops a righteousness as flawless and as meritorious as that of Christ. The second part involves the believer's performance, his behavior—*what he does*. According to the holy flesh concept, he can outgrow or neutralize his sinful nature so effectively that he is able to live as though he were no longer sinful, rendering perfect obedience to God's will. In other words, he learns to live without sinning.

The third part establishes *the deadline*—it marks the end of the time during which the believer must bring these two objectives to their full realization. That is, he must develop a flawless personal righteousness and learn to live without sinning before probation ends if he is to be among the redeemed who will be alive when Jesus comes. Should he fail to achieve his double goal, he has either to die before probation ends or else be lost for eternity.

The evidence shows that both Elder E. R. Jones and the holy flesh people employed certain "passages in the Testimonies" as the basis of their extreme views. They quoted some statements from Ellen White's writings that appeared to support their teachings. It is therefore extremely important to note that *when they used her writings to support the idea that before probation ends God's people can and must become sinless, pure, and holy like Jesus, she opposed them with a determination seldom seen in her long ministry for the church.*

Her reaction leads to at least the following conclusions: 1. We must recognize a radical difference between (a) being able to produce a few isolated passages from the Testimonies in support of a particular view and (b) developing a position that is indeed a reliable representation of Ellen White's teachings on a given subject. 2. If not rightly understood and properly applied some statements in the Testimonies can indeed lead someone to develop erroneous views such as those advocated by Elder E. R. Jones and his followers. The fact that they used her writings to authenticate their teachings bears this out.

3. Most of Ellen White's writings are short pieces—such as letters, articles, and manuscripts—written to particular audiences, within definite historical contexts, and with specific objectives in mind. It should therefore come as no surprise that when we compare them with one another we sometimes find certain ideological tensions not always easy to resolve. It is particularly a problem when we either ignore the conceptual and historical contexts or do not take the specific intent of particular passages into consideration.

Here, however, we are dealing with some specific teachings with which Ellen White was familiar, and that she condemned in unmistakable terms. To argue that Ellen White's writings endorse the very same views she so forcefully rejected as error, man-made tests, fallacy, and so forth, would be an absurd proposition indeed. We can therefore rest assured that whenever someone uses her writings to support views like those held by

Elder E. R. Jones and his followers, they are falsely interpreting, improperly using, and incorrectly applying the Testimonies.

4. Every individual has the right to decide for himself whether to accept or to reject the teachings presented by Elder Jones and his followers. However, in view of what we have seen, no one has the right to claim that such teachings represent either Ellen White's view or the position of the Adventist Church.

3. What Will Happen Shortly Before the Return of Christ

Besides condemning the teachings advocated by Elder Jones and rebuking him for misusing both Scripture and her writings, Ellen White also predicted that similar concepts would seek to infiltrate the Adventist Church again in the future. She said:

> I have been shown that deceptions like those we were called to meet in the early experiences of the message would be repeated, and that we shall have to meet them again in the closing days of the work (*Selected Messages*, book 2, p. 28). The things you have described as taking place in Indiana [the geographic center of the holy flesh movement], the Lord has shown me would take place just before the close of probation (*ibid.*, p. 36).

According to her, then, the deception that will attempt to corrupt God's message of mercy to the world, frustrate the mission of Adventism, and unsettle the religious experience of many of its members is not an overemphasis on the redemptive work finished on the cross—the event on the basis of which the believer now stands before the Father perfectly righteous in Christ by faith. As we have already seen, Ellen White places great emphasis upon Christ's role both as atoning sacrifice on the cross, where He absolved man's condemnation, and as representative advocate in the presence of the Father, where "He ceases not to present His people moment by moment, complete in Himself" *(Faith and Works,* p. 107).

The deception that no doubt will cause many to remain in their Laodicean condition is, rather, a repeat of the fanaticism that took place shortly after the 1844 disappointment, appeared again at the turn of the century, and revived in a more sophisticated form in the late 1950s. Since Satan is the master deceiver, we can anticipate that he will modify the most offensive aspects of this heresy and better disguise its most obvious features. But if Ellen White is correct, as we believe she is, its emphasis on the believer and his accomplishments—his personal righteousness and flawless obedience—as opposed to what the believer is in Christ by faith and what Christ does for him as his advocate with the Father, will be its most distinctive characteristic.

4. The Essence and Significance of the "New" Deception

It is almost axiomatic that a deception is not a complete denial or a direct contradiction but a distortion of truth. Its appeal as well as its power to delude lie precisely in the fact that it contains elements of truth. We shall therefore examine this "new" deception from two overall perspectives: First we will compare and contrast it with the counterfeit introduced by the human system of priesthood prevalent in part of the Christian church. Then we will discuss it in light of man's fall in the Garden of Eden.

a. An Attempt to Displace Christ as the Only Way to the Father

Although the new deception differs in approach from the old one that was so widespread throughout

Christendom for centuries, the new deception leads to basically the same negative results. They are both attempts to displace Christ, the divine high priest, by providing alternative ways to secure a right standing with God. Through its human system of priesthood, the old deception created a different access to the forgiveness and saving grace of God. As a result, not Jesus but the church became the saving link between the sinner and God. Through its theology of character development and behavior modification, the new deception, in turn, introduces another way—a new method—by which to meet the standard of perfect righteousness that God requires for salvation.

We have seen that the only way for a fallen being to be righteous in God's sight this side of glorification is by his partaking of the saving merits of the Saviour. Because in himself he is sinful, imperfect, and unworthy, the believer can be righteous only by faith in Christ. Jesus is the basis of his standing with God. Also, we have observed that the believer's salvation becomes permanently secure and God declares him worthy of eternal life at the pre-Advent judgment only because he has accepted Christ's redemptive mediation on his behalf. Jesus will complete His mediatorial role—He will fully achieve the purpose of His high-priestly ministry—by securing for the living believer God's final and irreversible verdict of acceptance as the pre-Advent judgment concludes.

In contrast, the new deception teaches that the believer develops in his own life a righteousness that is just as perfect and consequently as meritorious as that belonging to the Saviour. Because he supposedly becomes as pure, holy, and worthy as Jesus, it follows that the believer no longer depends on the imputed righteousness of Christ for his standing with God. As a result, his assurance of salvation no longer rests on the redemptive work of Christ on his behalf, but on the spiritual perfection and moral flawlessness he himself has achieved in his own life.

According to the new deception, the last generation of believers will win such a radical victory over sin and develop such a perfect righteousness in their own lives that the fact that Jesus ceases to mediate for them at the end of probation will have no adverse effect on them whatsoever. Since their characters are as righteous as that of Christ and their obedience is as perfect as His, they will stand before God as positively sinless, righteous, and worthy in themselves as they did earlier when Christ was still imputing His righteousness to them. The proponents of this view would probably deny it, but the fact is that the moment the believer achieves such a supposed state of total sanctification, he also transcends his need of Christ either as Saviour or as Mediator. His equality to Christ in righteousness also makes him equal to Christ in personal standing with the Father.

The new deception confronting the Adventist Church is an integral part of Satan's ongoing war against Christ. When he failed to displace Christ in heaven Satan continued the battle here on the earth. Through the fall of Adam and Eve he gained temporary rulership over the world. But that came to an end, in principle, when Christ—the second Adam and new head of mankind—died an atoning death on man's behalf. By His death He also destroyed the power of death and established God's kingdom of grace on Planet Earth. Since then Satan is a defeated foe whose eventual destruction is assured. But he has not ceased from his attempts to defeat Christ. He lost in heaven, and he lost on earth. But he can still win in the human heart, for he can still displace Christ there. And that is precisely what he is endeavoring to do.

For the most part, Satan's strategy has not been direct confrontation, but subtle deception and counterfeit. For example, when God employed the sacrificial system to illustrate His work in Christ for the redemption of man, the devil did not attack the idea of reconciliation with God. Instead, Satan introduced a wide variety of different means and methods by which mankind supposedly can achieve such reconciliation, and he concentrated on leading sinners to attempt to find favor with God by means of his counterfeits instead of placing their faith in Christ.

Needless to say, in the lives of men Satan has been extremely successful in pushing Christ aside as the only channel to God. And he has been most successful with religious people by convincing them to continue trying to eliminate sin—the cause of their alienation from God—instead of availing themselves of the redemptive work of Christ. It really means that they approach their predicament as lost sinners as though there were no Saviour. They endeavor to solve their sin problem on their own instead of accepting the solution God has already provided in Christ.

The new deception appeals to religious people precisely because it promises freedom from sin—something for which all true believers long with great desire. The problem is that when they seek to achieve a right standing with God through their own moral and spiritual accomplishments, they become "alienated from Christ," their only link of spiritual unity with God, and fall "away from grace" (Gal. 5:4). As a result, (1) they lose access to the benefits of Christ's redemptive work, and with it the right, conferred by grace at conversion, to continue as members of God's spiritual family of believers. And (2) they revert to the state of lostness, enmity, and condemnation in which they found themselves before their reconciliation took place.

Thus, under the guise of the enticing and apparently commendable objective of partaking of the divine nature and achieving sinless perfection—just like Jesus—the new deception nullifies the membership of religious people in God's covenant of grace and places them squarely under the yoke of the covenant of works. As a result, they end up attempting to achieve salvation through a method that has no access to God's forgiveness, the saving righteousness of Christ, the enabling power of the Spirit, and any other of the gifts that, according to Scripture, God makes available only to those who retain their status as His sons and daughters through their continual faith relationship with Jesus Christ (see Luke 24:45-47; Acts 2:38; Rom. 8:9, etc.).

b. An Enticement to Eliminate Some Basic Distinctions Between Jesus and Sinners

The deception confronting the Adventist Church is not really new. In fact, it is but a refinement and adaptation of the one that caused humanity's fall in the Garden of Eden. According to the biblical description, *the first deception introduced a radical change into God's plan in the creation of man.* The first human sin was not a failure to live up to the high moral demands of a legal code. Nor was it a plunging down toward the evil and perverse—something that one could call a sin of the flesh, such as adultery, murder, or stealing. Instead, it was a sin of the spirit, a reaching higher than what the Creator had ordained.

Creation established a clear and permanent distinction between the divine and the human. Because God created man in His image, there was a considerable resemblance and closeness between the Creator and the creature. But the fact that man was created an image, or representation, of God and not a true counterpart also indicates that, in the Creator's order, God is God and man is man, and there will forever remain an essential difference and an unbreachable distance between the two.

In a forthcoming book on the biblical concept of man, I shall deal with this subject in depth. For our purpose here, suffice it to say that because God had created them in His image, Adam and Eve could reflect in their own personhood the righteous attributes and noble virtues of the holy character of God. They were spiritually complete because their unhindered spiritual union with the Creator made them direct participants in His goodness, righteousness, and holiness. But because they were only an image of God, and not God in essence, they were dependent on the Creator, who alone ultimately possesses such positive virtues.

When the deceiver tempted Adam and Eve with the thought of becoming "like God" (Gen. 3:5), he awoke in them the desire to reach a level that was different from the Creator's purpose for man—to enjoy a level of existence higher than what God intended for them to attain. The first deception enticed humanity to seek to eliminate the radical qualitative difference that distinguishes the divine from the human and separates the Creator from the creature. Man's first sin was a refusal to accept his creatureliness—a presumptuous attempt to transcend the limitations of his finite status and attain to the self-determination and autosufficiency that belongs to God alone.

As a branch cannot exist by itself but depends on the vine to live, grow, and produce fruit, so original man dependent on God to be and do what the Creator meant he should be and do. *Man's first sin was an attempt to outgrow his status as "branch" and to become a "vine" instead.* He sought to be and to have in himself that which, according to the Creator's plan, he could be and have only as he continually partook of what orginates with God and therefore is His exclusive possession.

Obviously, humanity's first sin was in essence a refusal to be and to live by the grace of God. Instead of continuing to reflect in their own person what proceeds from the Creator, Adam and Eve attempted to be what they were—good, righteous, holy—in and by them-selves, even as God is. Man the image of God wanted to be man essentially God by experiencing an inner trans-formation in nature that would enable him to become a full participant in both the status and the nature of God.

By comparison, *the new deception introduces a change in the plan God devised for human redemption.* Representing a level that is higher than and different from what God has established in Scripture, the deception seeks to achieve spiritual equality with the God-man, Jesus Christ. Those enticed by it are not satisfied that, by God's grace, imperfect believers—growing sons and daughters of God—become blameless, righteous, and holy through the saving righteousness of Christ. In-stead, they want to experience an inner transformation that somehow will enable them to transcend their sinful condition and to become perfectly faultless, righteous, and holy *in themselves,* even as Christ is.

To strive to be the best person one can possibly be at every stage of his spiritual growth, and to increasingly pattern his life after what is true and right and loving, is a commendable and scripturally sound endeavor. It is my contention, however, that *there is a radical difference between trying to live as is worthy of God's sons and daughters in Christ and attempting to equal, match, and duplicate in one's own life the absolute righteousness of Christ, the divine-human Son of God.* To endeavor to be more like Jesus in character and conduct is one thing, while to attempt to be just as righteous and holy as He was during His life on earth is quite another. The former is an objective based on God's word as recorded in Scripture. The latter is an arrogant departure from it, and therefore constitutes sin.

It is important to note that in both its old and new forms, the appeal of the deception—and also its sin—lies in the fact that it presents an objective that, at least on the surface, appears to be commendable. Since by definition God is the supreme good of the universe, it logically follows that there could exist no higher ideal or nobler objective for Adam and Eve than endeavoring to be just like Him. Yet—and here is the irony—because the deception represents an attempt to breach the distance between the creature and the Creator, to merge the human with the divine, and to erase the qualitative difference between the eternal and self-sufficient I AM and dependent, mortal man, it constituted *sin* of the highest order.

The same problem is true with the believer's relationship to Jesus Christ. Obviously Jesus is the perfect example, the highest ideal that could possibly be set before the believer. We must not forget, however, that although He became man, Jesus never ceased to be God. While it is true that He took humanity upon Himself, it is also true that He never gave up His divinity. As "the Holy and Righteous One" (Acts 3:14), He is the personification of perfect goodness, absolute righteousness, and total holiness. Jesus veiled His infinite glory and relinquished the active use of His unlimited power, but He never yielded the flawless moral qualities and holy spiritual attributes that enabled Him to reveal the Father's righteous character to fallen man.

Scripture establishes the fact that "in Christ all the fullness of the Deity lives in bodily form" (Col. 2:9). He who "was God" "became flesh and made his dwelling among us. We have seen his glory, the glory of the One and Only, who came from the Father, full of grace and truth" (John 1:1,14). Jesus "is the radiance of God's glory and the exact representation of his being" (Heb. 1:3). Ellen White rightly states:

> The Lord Jesus took upon Him the form of sinful man, clothing His divinity with humanity. But *He was holy, even as God is holy*. If He had not been without spot or stain of sin, He could not have been the Saviour of mankind. He was a Sin-bearer, needing no atonement. *One with God in purity and holiness of character,* He could make a propitiation for the sins of the whole world (*This Day With God,* p. 357; italics supplied).

So when someone endeavors to develop in his own personal life a righteousness that is as perfect—and consequently as meritorious—as that of Christ, he does more than just attempt to equal the outstanding spiritual achievements of the only perfect Man who ever lived on earth since the Fall. He is striving to eliminate all distinction between the Saviour and the sinners He came to save. He is seeking to erase the difference and bridge the distance between himself and the Son of God, who, being just as pure, righteous, and holy as God the Father, needed no mediator, but lived in direct and unhindered spiritual unity with the other two Persons of the Godhead.

We therefore conclude that the new deception is essentially the same as the one that caused man's fall in the beginning. *As the first deception enticed man to transcend his state and achieve equality with the Creator, so the last deception allures the believer to outgrow his sinful condition and achieve equality with the Saviour.*

As a result of Satan's deception, Adam and Eve became dissatisfied with having to depend on the Creator for continuing to be man in the image of God, and attempted to be righteous, holy, and good in and by themselves, even as God is. In turn, those who yield to the new deception are not content to depend on Christ for their standing with God, but attempt to be righteous, holy, and good in themselves, even as Christ is.

Unfortunately, the consequences of yielding to the new deception are as radical and as tragic as those of yielding to the first temptation. Under the guise of the apparently noble objective of granting them equality with God, the first deception disrupted our first parents' primal relationship with their Creator. It caused their spiritual separation from Him who alone could enable them to continue reflecting the righteous virtues of God's holy character in their personal lives. As a result, they lost their original spiritual wholeness and fell into a state of lostness, alienation, and sin.

So it is with the new deception. Lurking beneath the apparently noble objective of granting believers spiritual equality with Jesus, it disrupts their faith relationship with the Saviour. It spiritually divorces them from Him who alone can present them to the Father perfectly righteous and grant them the right to inherit eternal life. As a result, they lose their participation in the benefits of the covenant of grace and fall back into the state of lostness, condemnation, and death that is the predicament of all fallen beings outside of Christ.

VII Two Groups of People in the Church: Those Righteous in Christ by Faith and Those Unrighteous

Finally, we will consider some statements in Ellen White's writings that indicate that the church contains only two kinds of people: (1) those who are righteous because they are covered in the merits of the Saviour and (2) those who are unrighteous because they attempt to meet God's standard of perfect righteousness "independent of the atonement" and "without the virtue of divine mediation."

According to Ellen White, the two classes have their first representatives in Cain and Abel, and will coexist in the church to the end of time:

> The Pharisee and the publican represent two great classes into which those who come to worship God are divided. Their first two representatives are found in the first two children that were born into the world. Cain thought himself righteous, and he came to God with a thank offering only. He made no confession of sin, and acknowledged no need of mercy. But Abel came with the blood that pointed to the Lamb of God. He came as a sinner, confessing himself lost; his only hope was the unmerited love of God (*Christ's Object Lessons,* p. 152).

> "By faith Abel offered unto God a more excellent sacrifice than Cain" (Heb. 11:4). Abel grasped the great principles of redemption. He saw himself a sinner. . . .

149

Through the shed blood [of a lamb] he looked to the future sacrifice, Christ dying on the cross of Calvary; and trusting in the atonement that was there to be made, he had the witness that he was righteous, and his offering accepted. . . . Cain and Abel represent two classes that will exist in the world till the close of time. One class avail themselves of the appointed sacrifice for sin; the other venture to depend upon their own merits; theirs is a sacrifice without the virtue of divine mediation, and thus it is not able to bring man into favor with God. . . .

Those who feel no need of the blood of Christ, who feel that without divine grace they can by their own works secure the approval of God, are making the same mistake as did Cain. If they do not accept the cleansing blood, they are under condemnation. There is no other provision made whereby they can be released from the thralldom of sin. . . . As Cain thought to secure the divine favor by an offering that lacked the blood of a sacrifice, so do these expect to exalt humanity to the divine standard, independent of the atonement (*Patriarchs and Prophets*, pp. 72, 73).

We will look at three specific concepts: 1. Cain understood neither his real predicament as a fallen being nor the dynamics of the salvation God provided in the Substitute. In his spiritual blindness he thought himself to be righteous, not realizing he was a lost, guilty, and unworthy sinner. Consequently he approached God with a thank offering only. He made no confession of sin, he brought no atoning blood, he acknowledged no need of mercy. As a result, he had no access either to God's forgiveness or to the Saviour's merits that Christ mediates only to those who come to God claiming His redemptive work on their behalf.

2. Abel realized his true condition as a fallen being and grasped the great principles of redemption. He went to God as a sinner, confessing himself lost, and

placed his faith in and based his hope on the unmerited love of God as manifested in the atonement Christ would make at the cross on his behalf. By faith he brought the sacrifice God had stipulated—the blood that pointed to the Lamb of God. That is the basis—the only basis—for the witness that he was righteous, and the reason his offering was accepted.

3. The church—"those who come to worship God"—contains two distinct categories of people. One group—represented by Cain and the Pharisee in Christ's parable—consists of religious moralists who are spiritually self-sufficient. They do not recognize their own sinfulness and therefore come to God with a thank offering only—an offering that lacks the cleansing blood of Christ's sacrifice and is independent of the atonement. Their offering does not have the virtue of divine mediation and, consequently, cannot give them access to God. In their Laodicean blindness they do not perceive their moral inadequacy and spiritual destitution. As a result, they have no desire to repent, and feel no need to open the door to Christ as their only source of saving righteousness.

The other group within the church—represented by Abel and the tax collector in Christ's parable—is made up of those who understand both their predicament as fallen beings and the great principles of redemption. They know that except for the salvation God has provided in Christ, they are as lost, guilty, and helpless as any other sinner. That is why they avail themselves of Christ's redemptive work on their behalf and, by faith, cover their spiritual nakedness with the robe of His all-sufficient righteousness. Like Abel they have the witness that they are righteous, the true children of God through faith in Jesus Christ.

It is important to note that the criterion determining the separation of the church into two groups is not achievement-centered but Christ-centered. In other words, the church does not divide into one segment who are righteous in themselves and have learned to live without sinning, and another who failed to reach this double objective. Instead, the church separates into those who avail themselves of Christ's redemptive work on their behalf and therefore are righteous in Christ by faith, and those who make their own spiritual accomplishments the ultimate basis of their standing and consequently have nothing to bring them into favor with God.

Notice how Ellen White elsewhere expresses the same concept:

> The Pharisee felt no conviction of sin. The Holy Spirit could not work with him. His soul was encased in a self-righteous armor which the arrows of God, barbed and true-aimed by angel hands, failed to penetrate. It is only he who knows himself to be a sinner that Christ can save (*Christ's Object Lessons*, p. 158).

> Self-righteousness is the danger of this age; it separates the soul from Christ. *Those who trust to their own righteousness cannot understand how salvation comes through Christ (Faith and Works*, p. 96; italics supplied). There is nothing so offensive to God or so dangerous to the human soul as pride and self-sufficiency. Of all sins it is the most hopeless, the most incurable (*Christ's Object Lessons*, p. 154).

> Let those who feel inclined to make a high profession of holiness look into the mirror of God's law. As they see its far-reaching claims, and understand its work as a discerner of the thoughts and intents of the heart, they will not boast of sinlessness (*The Acts of the Apostles*, p. 562).

152

How can anyone who is brought before the holy standard of God's law—which makes apparent the evil motives, the unhallowed desires, the infidelity of the heart, the impurity of the lips, and that lays bare the life—make any boast of holiness? His acts of disloyalty in making void the law of God are exposed to his sight, and his spirit is stricken and afflicted under the searching influence of the Spirit of God. He loathes himself, as he views the greatness, the majesty, the pure and spotless character of Jesus Christ (Ellen G. White, in *Review and Herald*, Oct. 16, 1888).

There is nothing in us from which we can clothe the soul so that its nakedness shall not appear. We are to receive the robe of righteousness woven in the loom of heaven, even the spotless robe of Christ's righteousness (*ibid.*, July 19, 1892). Nothing is apparently more helpless, yet really more invincible, than the soul that feels its nothingness and relies wholly on the merits of the Saviour (*The Ministry of Healing*, p. 182).

No man can look within himself and find anything in his character that will recommend him to God, or make his acceptance sure. It is only through Jesus, whom the Father gave for the life of the world, that the sinner may find access to God. Jesus alone is our Redeemer, our Advocate and Mediator; in Him is our only hope for pardon, peace, and righteousness (*Selected Messages*, book 1, pp. 332, 333).

Since the considerations in this chapter arise from the stories of Cain and Abel, and the Pharisee and the tax collector in Christ's parable, we will briefly examine and discuss the scriptural account of the two cases.

1. Cain and Abel Offer Sacrifices to God

Scripture says little about the circumstances surrounding the incident when Cain and Abel brought their respective sacrifices to God. However, when we examine the implications of Cain's act of bringing "some of the fruits of the soil as an offering to the Lord" (Gen. 4:3), we can draw several conclusions with a reasonable degree of certainty:

First, at least to some extent, Cain recognized his fallen condition and wanted reconciliation with God—otherwise it is difficult to see why he should have brought God a sacrifice at all. Second, he obeyed God in building an altar and bringing an offering. His problem was that he had the wrong sacrifice—one that, instead of representing faith in the Substitute, symbolized dependence on one's own efforts for his standing with God.

Third, apparently Cain ignored the fact that only Christ's righteousness can accomplish man's reconciliation with God. He failed to understand that *when it comes to our personal standing with God, nothing less than the Saviour's perfect merits is sufficient, nothing equally meritorious is possible, and nothing else is acceptable to God.* Since "without the shedding of blood there is no forgiveness" (Heb. 9:22), nothing a sinner can grow in his own garden can take the place of the Lamb that God provided as a means to bring man back into favor with Him. The fruit Cain brought was probably the very best he had to offer, and it all grew through the power of God. But it symbolized man's accomplishments, accomplishments that, having no redemptive value, do not belong on the altar.

Fourth, Cain's behavior indicates quite persuasively that *while he accepted the idea of reconciliation* with God—and to some extent showed he wanted to live in good terms with Him—*he rejected the means* God provided in Christ to make both reconciliation and a right relationship possible. Because Cain's fruit represented a change in God's plan to redeem His lost children, his offering

154

not only failed to achieve its intended purpose but also increased his guilt and alienation from God.

Fifth, God did not reject Cain because he was a sinner. God knew the man's lost condition, and that is precisely why He provided a solution to his sin problem. The Lord could not accept Cain and his offering, because he did not place his faith in the Substitute God provided as the only means of salvation.

> By faith Abel offered God a better sacrifice than Cain did. By faith he was commended as a righteous man, when God spoke well of his offerings. And by faith he still speaks, even though he is dead (Heb. 11:4).

Abel's offering was "better" because (1) it was the one God had stipulated as a symbol of Christ, and because (2) he brought it "by faith." He was "commended as a righteous man," not because he was morally blameless and spiritually perfect, but because through his sacrifice he showed his faith in the atoning blood of Christ for forgiveness, and his dependence on Christ's infinite merits for a right standing with God.

2. Pharisee and Tax Collector Pray in the Temple

According to Jesus' parable recorded in Luke 18:9-14, a Pharisee and a tax collector went up to the Temple to pray. They were both religious men—church members, we would probably say in our modern terminology. The Pharisee thanked God for being a better person and having a better behavioral record than "other men" who, according to him, were "robbers, evildoers, adulterers." In contrast, the tax collector recognized himself a sinner and prayed to God for mercy.

Since Jesus did not contradict the Pharisee's self-evaluation, we can conclude that he spoke the truth when he said he did not rob or commit adultery as did other men. He probably also had long and detailed records to prove he fasted twice a week and paid faithful tithe. So his problem was not that he was a chronic sinner who lived in deliberate and open violation to the will of God. Instead, it was that because he thought himself righteous he felt no need of a Saviour.

The Pharisee's spiritual predicament resulted from two theological misunderstandings: First, he apparently defined man's sin problem only in terms of moral character and ethical behavior. In his view, only wicked people who expressed open rebellion against God by willfully breaking the letter of the law were guilty of sin. Therefore he felt quite good about himself. Because he was not evil and immoral as he perceived other men to be, he thought he had a good moral character that deserved God's approval. Having not broken any specific prohibition of the law—such as robbing and adultery—he assumed that he had rendered perfect obedience and was therefore free of guilt. And because he believed that he had evidence to prove he fulfilled his religious duties—such as fasting twice a week and paying an accurate tithe—he concluded that he was positively righteous, truly worthy of God's approval.

Second, the Pharisee had a righteousness-by-works conception of salvation. That is, he based his standing with God—and by extension his assurance of eternal life—on his personal moral goodness and behavioral flawlessness. Such a view ruled out two things: (1) God's grace in providing the Substitute to pay the penalty for his guilt, cancel his death sentence, and give him the right to become a child of God, and (2) the believer's response of repentance and faith by which he would become a participant in the Saviour's redemptive activity—a work that would grant him God's forgiveness and make him worthy of eternal life through the imputed righteousness of Christ.

TWO GROUPS OF PEOPLE

According to the parable, the Pharisee's visit to the Temple brought him no blessing, and he returned home unchanged. He was a morally righteous man—a man with deep religious commitment, a great regard for the law, and a high standard of ethical behavior. But he was also someone who in his spiritual pride and religious self-sufficiency did not realize his desperate need of a Saviour. That is, he felt no need for either God's forgiveness or the imputed righteousness of Christ. Although he had obeyed the law—in a sense—he ignored the gospel. As a result, he had no access to God's covenant of grace, no part in Christ and the salvation He alone provides. So he went home convinced that according to the law he was righteous, but unaware that according to the gospel he was lost.

The tax collector's experience was the exact opposite of what happened to the Pharisee. The prayer of the taxgatherer indicates that he recognized himself a sinner and based his hope for a right standing with God on His mercy. Because in repentance he surrendered what he was and because in faith he accepted what God's grace provides, he "went home justified before God" (Luke 18:14). He came to the Temple a lost, guilty, and hopeless sinner, but returned to his home fully reconciled to God, a son of God in Christ, an heir to eternal life. Should he have died—or should probation have ended—at that point in time his eternal salvation would have been secure in Christ. The publican would have participated at the wedding feast of the Lamb and had part in God's eternal kingdom of glory, not because he no longer was a sinner, but because he now had a Saviour, and consequently stood before God totally forgiven and perfectly righteous in Christ by faith.

VIII Summary and Conclusions

This chapter has two general sections. The first one provides a summary of some of the major points we discussed in the preceding seven chapters. The second section contains some overall conclusions based on the concepts we derived from Ellen White's writings.

A. Summary

The first chapter examined two basic concepts and some of their major ramifications. First, we saw that the believer totally depends upon Christ for a right standing with the Father because God requires perfect righteousness, and man is incapable of producing it. Second, we saw that Jesus mediates for the believer to present him—as an individual person—perfectly righteous before the Father. Jesus imputes His atoning death, His redemptive victory, and His saving righteousness to the believer so that he may stand by faith before God faultless in Christ.

In order to enable Christ to act as his substitute, the believer must respond to the gospel in repentance and faith. Through repentance the believer indicates that he recognizes both his guilt and the inadequacy of what he is, what he has, and what he does to secure God's approval. Through faith he acknowledges his inability to bring himself into favor with God, and therefore avails himself of Christ's redemptive work on his behalf. Thus the believer gains access to God's forgiveness for his sin and to Christ's perfect righteousness for acceptance with the Father.

SUMMARY AND CONCLUSIONS

Since sanctification is a process never totally finished in the present life, the believer never becomes righteous in himself, but can be so only in Christ for as long as he lives. All he is and all he has, as a son of God, he is and he has only because and for as long as he partakes of Christ by faith. Should he ever lose his hold on Christ— and in so doing cease to participate in His redemptive work—the believer would revert to the state of lostness, condemnation, and death in which he found himself before his reconciliation took place at conversion.

In the second chapter we saw that the believer also depends on Christ's mediation to make his life as a child of God acceptable to the Father. God requires not just obedience but perfect obedience, and that the believer is incapable of providing. The believer's obedience has no value with God, first, because it is partial and imperfect and therefore deserves not divine approval but condemnation, and second, because the believer's sinful nature defiles everything he does and thus renders it unacceptable to God.

We also made a distinction between true obedience—or the obedience of faith—and perfect obedience. True obedience includes submission to the injunctions of the law and compliance with the demands of the gospel. Consequently the truly obedient are those who, having done their best to live as is worthy of the sons and daughters of God in Christ, recognize their sinfulness, imperfection, and unworthiness, and approach the Father in repentance and faith. Christ's atoning blood then cleanses them of their guilt, and His saving righteousness preserves them in a right standing with God.

The fact that we are sinners defiles our obedience. Nothing that sinful beings can render to God is acceptable on its own merits. It is satisfactory only when—and by virtue of the fact that—we bring it to the Father through the merits of the Son. Perfect obedience is therefore possible only through Christ's mediation on our behalf. When we depend on Christ's redemptive work for our standing with God, our divine High Priest imputes the Saviour's righteousness to us in order to make up for our deficiencies and render our obedience, our service, and our worship perfectly pleasing to the Father.

In the third chapter we recognized that no fallen being has ever reached the goal of unblemished spiritual perfection outside of Christ. The patriarchs, prophets, and apostles—men who lived the nearest to God—admitted their sinfulness. Their unusually close relationship with God enabled them to acquire both the point of reference and the spiritual perception needed to see themselves as they really were. Therefore they all knew that nothing they were, nothing they had, and nothing they did could secure them God's favor.

Since all have sinned and fallen short of the glory of God, all humans alike—from Abel, the first believer to die, to the last sinner to accept God's saving grace in Christ just before probation ends—depend equally on Christ's redemptive work for salvation. Because God devised a plan of redemption according to which Jesus Christ—His atoning death, redemptive victory, and saving righteousness imputed to the believer by faith—is the only way to the Father, all humans will either be saved by God's undeserved grace or be lost.

The fourth chapter discussed the idea that an individual's perception of his spiritual condition—whether he sees himself as righteous and good or imperfect and sinful—results from his relative spiritual closeness to Jesus and the adequacy of his view of the perfection of Christ. Those who do not have a close and enlightened faith relationship with Jesus lack both the point of reference and the spiritual eyesight that would enable them to see their moral inadequacy and spiritual imperfection. They underestimate their sinfulness and overestimate their possibilities. As a result they do not sense their total dependence on Christ.

Those who live nearest to Jesus have at least the following characteristics: 1. They have come to appreciate the beauty of Christ's holy character, and therefore see their own sinfulness. 2. They have a clear understanding of the far-reaching nature of God's requirements, and therefore realize how far they really are from meeting the standard He requires for salvation. 3. They adequately sense the terribleness of sin and of the frailty and sinfulness of humanity, and therefore know their total dependence on Christ. 4. They live in a state of "continual repentance and faith in the blood of Christ," fully aware that their salvation depends, not on their own goodness, but on God's infinite grace.

We also saw that, according to Ellen White, the remnant church does not reach sinless perfection of either being or conduct by the time probation ends. Its members are not supersaints who have fully attained and therefore stand in flawless righteousness before the tribunal of God. On the contrary, they are sinners who, save for Christ's righteousness, have nothing but "filthy garments" to wear. Painfully aware of "the sinfulness of their lives, . . . their weakness and unworthiness," "their defective characters," "their unlikeness to Christ," they "afflict their souls" in repentance before God "on account of their own transgressions," and plead for a "purity of heart" they obviously do not yet possess.

Should God decide the eternal destiny of the remnant church on the basis of their true spiritual condition and actual moral behavior, their case would be hopeless.

Fortunately Jesus, the powerful mediator, silences the accuser with arguments founded, not upon the believers' own merits—for they have none—but upon their dependence on His redemptive activity on their behalf. He removes their filthy garments and covers them with the glorious robe of His spotless righteousness and thus presents them to the Father righteous in Christ.

The fifth chapter looked at some of the most significant events connected with the end of probation and the time of trouble. Some of the major concepts discussed were as follows: First, Jesus will continue His mediatorial ministry until He achieves its intended purpose fully and completely. That is, He will cease to act as man's advocate with the Father only after He has God's final and irreversible verdict of approval for His people as the pre-Advent judgment closes. As a result, they receive "the seal of the living God," which grants their sonship in Christ a permanent status, and bestows upon them the right to be heirs of the kingdom.

Second, the moment when Jesus completes His mediation for the last generation of believers also marks the end of the pre-Advent judgment. The "final test" that determines eternal destinies "has been brought upon the world. . . . The number of His subjects is made up." The future of all is permanently and irrevocably fixed, each case not only decided but forever closed, never more to be opened for revision. Because the decision that God pronounces as the judgment concludes is final, those who will be saved are saved, and those who will be lost are lost *as of that moment*.

Third, at least three major factors give the believers peace, assurance, and hope as they face the end of probation and the time of trouble: 1. Jesus will mediate in their behalf until God's final verdict of acceptance has made their salvation permanently sure. 2. They will not have to face an after-judgment test to determine whether or not they have achieved flawless righteousness of being and sinlessness of conduct and hence are personally worthy of eternal life. 3. God will protect and provide for them during the short period of time between the end of probation and the second coming of Christ, so that nothing will jeopardize their salvation.

Fourth, the time of trouble will be a period of deep spiritual intensity, sincere self-examination, and earnest wrestling with God. The experience of God's people during this time seeks to achieve three basic objectives: (1) to demonstrate that they have sincerely repented of their sin and trust in God's forgiveness; (2) to lead them to a full realization of their unworthiness to have a part in God's kingdom of glory; and (3) to strengthen their faith that God will fulfill the gospel promises to them in spite of their shortcomings, imperfection, and sinfulness.

The sixth chapter explored a peculiar deception that entered Adventism shortly after the 1844 disappointment, appeared again at the turn of the century, revived in a more sophisticated form in the late 1950s, and, according to Ellen White, will confront the church again before the end of probation. Judging by its past influence, this "message of error" has the potential to corrupt God's message of mercy to the world, frustrate the mission of Adventism, and unsettle the religious experience of many of its members.

Such "fanaticism" represents a radical departure from the teachings of Scripture and obviously contradicts most of the significant concepts we have derived from the writings of Ellen White. 1. It changes the standard the last generation must meet for salvation and also the method by which believers can achieve it. 2. It modifies Christ's role as Saviour as well as the manner in which He saves. 3. It alters Christ's high-priestly ministry in heaven and greatly reduces the significance of His ongoing mediation with the Father. 4. It erases the essential distinction the Scriptures establish between the holy and righteous Son of God and the guilty sinners He came to save.

In the seventh chapter we found that the church will contain two radically different groups of people until the end of time. One group consists of those who do not realize their true spiritual condition and do not understand the great principles of redemption. They seek to be right with God by eliminating sin from their lives—and thus cease to be sinners—instead of accepting the solution to their sin problem that God has provided in Christ. By not coming to the Father, trusting solely in the merits of the Son, they have no access to the benefits of Christ's redemptive work. As a result, they remain in the state of lostness, guilt, and eventual eternal death that is the common destiny of all sinful beings outside of Christ.

The other group includes only those who understand both their real predicament as fallen beings and the dynamics of the plan of redemption. They know that, as God reviews their cases to determine their eternal destiny, nothing less than the imputed righteousness of Christ is sufficient, nothing equally adequate is possible, and nothing else is acceptable. Thus they depend entirely on the Saviour's atoning death, redemptive victory and saving merits for their position with God. As a result, they stand before God righteous in Christ by faith, and continue enjoying their status, as adopted sons and daughters of God in Christ, that gives them the right to inherit eternal life.

B. Conclusions

One of the most attractive characteristics of the preceding concepts in Ellen White's writings is that they portray a scenario in which everything that has a bearing on the sinner's relationship with God occupies the place and carries out the function so clearly assigned to it in Scripture. We will briefly describe this scenario by outlining some of the most significant aspects of the role played by the Holy Spirit, the law of God, the believer, and Jesus Christ.

1. The Holy Spirit

Three of the Spirit's functions are particularly relevant here: The first one deals with the believer's behavior—his life as an adopted child of God. The Spirit helps him to gain an increasing understanding of God's will for man, on the one hand, and of the multifaceted and deceptive nature of sin, on the other. Gradually the Spirit increases the believer's spiritual capacity to differentiate between what is true and good and loving and what is not. He moves the believer to accept God's will as normative and to endeavor to pattern his life in harmony with it. And He enables the believer to do what only God knows is reasonable to expect of him at every advancing step of his growth and maturity.

The second major function of the Spirit relates to the believer's being—his nature and character. The Spirit keeps the believer's sinful nature under supernatural control so that it may not assert its evil desires and cause him to sever his spiritual union with Christ and rebel against God. The Spirit makes him willing to continue his struggle to overcome his sinful character traits, tendencies, and attitudes. And He enables the believer to develop a personal character that increasingly reflects the holy traits and righteous virtues of the perfect character of Christ.

The last major function of the Spirit we will mention has to do with the believer's faith relationship with Jesus Christ as his personal Saviour and only source of saving righteousness. The Spirit protects the believer from falling away from grace by helping him to develop the spiritual eyesight he needs to constantly recognize his shortcomings and imperfections, and his consequent need of Christ. The Spirit strengthens the believer's spiritual union with the Saviour and motivates him to live in a state of repentance and faith so that through Christ he may continue having access to God's grace and retain the right to be a child of God and an heir to eternal life.

It is important to note that the Spirit's role is not to work in competition against Christ by creating an alternative way for a sinner to achieve a right standing with God independent of Christ's mediation. Nowhere does Scripture affirm—or even remotely suggest—that one of the Spirit's functions is to help the believer to transcend his sinful condition, to outgrow his spiritual destitution and moral imperfection, and to develop a personal righteousness that is as perfect and as meritorious as Christ's. Instead, the Spirit keeps the believer constantly depending on Christ's redemptive work.

2. The Law of God.

The scenario portrayed in Ellen White's writings reinforces the biblical concept that God did not intend that the law be another way of salvation—a means by which the sinner can develop flawless righteousness and earn merit with God. Instead, the law serves four basic purposes: 1. It provides specific principles that help sinful beings understand God's distinction between right and wrong, good and evil, loving and unloving behavior. 2. It prescribes the believer's conduct particularly in relation to God and to his fellowmen. 3. It serves as the moral standard according to which God judges our lives. 4. And by revealing our shortcomings and failures to live in total harmony with God's will, it makes us aware of our guilt and leads us to come to Christ for forgiveness and saving righteousness.

3. The Believer

The scenario we have described in this book views the believer as a sinner reconciled to God through faith in Christ and adopted into God's spiritual family of believers. His faith relationship to Jesus entitles him to sonship, and his sonship gives him the right to be an heir of the kingdom. Throughout his entire life the believer partakes of two radically different realities at one and the same time. Apart from Christ—in himself, by nature—he is sinful, guilty, unworthy. However, in Christ—by partaking of Him and His redemptive work by faith—he is righteous, faultless, and worthy of eternal life. In other words, the believer is still guilty but no longer condemned, still sinful but no longer lost.

Throughout his life as a child of God, the believer experiences character development, behavior modification, and spiritual growth and maturation that are real and significant. But because the redemptive process was not designed to come to complete realization during the present life, the believer never fully outgrows his personal sinfulness and never transcends his need of Christ this side of glorification. Only when the eternal replaces the temporal, when God's kingdom of glory becomes a concrete historical reality, and when God finally makes His children to be like Jesus "when he appears" (1 John 3:2; cf. Heb. 11:39, 40; Phil. 1:6) will the believer regain the original perfection that God created man with in the beginning. Then he will, for the first time ever, be faultless in himself by nature, just as our first parents were before the Fall. In the meantime the believer can be righteous, holy, and worthy only in Christ.

4. Jesus Christ

The Saviour stands tall, unchallenged, and unequaled at the very center of God's plan for human redemption. Scripture describes Him as "the author and perfecter of our faith" (Heb. 12:2). He is the only way back to the Father, and the only basis for our right standing with God. Yesterday Jesus died on the cross as our substitute to atone for our sin, free us from our guilt, and cancel our death sentence. Today He ministers for us on His heavenly throne to grant us eternal life by imputing to us His atoning death, redemptive victory, and saving righteousness, and thus presenting us perfectly acceptable to the Father. Tomorrow He will come again to complete our redemption by removing our sinfulness and restoring us to the perfect spiritual wholeness that man had at Creation. As a result of this transformation, we will reflect the image of God in our being as fully as did Adam and Eve before the Fall. Restored to complete spiritual unity with God, we will live perfect lives in the personal presence of our righteous, holy, and gracious Redeemer.

Then the Creator's initial plan of a righteous world inhabited by healthy, happy, and holy beings will finally come to its complete and permanent realization, thanks to the redemption God provided in Christ. The marks in the hands of Jesus and the white robes the redeemed wear throughout eternity will forever remind them that it was His atoning sacrifice at the cross on their behalf that saved them from eternal death, and His perfect righteousness imputed to them by faith that gave them access to eternal life. That is why gratitude will dominate heaven —joyful gratitude, expressed in endless praise to God, because His grace proved to be infinitely greater than human sin. Realizing that, all the redeemed of all ages will be equally ready to cast their golden crowns at the Saviour's feet, and eagerly join the universal choir singing:

> To him who sits on the throne and to the Lamb
> be praise and honor and glory and power,
> for ever and ever! (Rev. 5:13).

Appendix
Ellen White Statements That Appear to Support Perfectionism

We made at least three assertions in this book that require further elaboration: 1. In the introduction we stated that although Ellen White wrote much on the topic of the mediation of Christ, she did not always do so systematically or as clearly as one might wish. Consequently some statements are susceptible to being misunderstood. Therefore it should come as no surprise if individuals use them to support views that, instead of centering on Christ and His redemptive ministry in heaven, focus primarily on man and his meager achievements here on earth.

2. In the sixth chapter we indicated that Ellen White rebuked Elder E. R. Jones for using her writings to bolster the idea that before the end of probation God's people can and must reach the condition where they are perfectly righteous in themselves and learn to live without sinning. Some time later she did the same to others, such as S. S. Davis and R. S. Donnell, who advocated similar ideas. 3. And we said that some statements if not rightly understood and properly applied can indeed lead to the type of erroneous views presented by Jones and others.

It is important to note at the outset that usually three factors combine to lead to a misinterpretation of a given passage. The first relates to what the passage actually says. For whatever reason, the wording is not precise enough, and therefore the reader can interpret it in more than one way. The second factor has to do with what the researcher brings to the text—his presuppositions and prior understanding of the subject. His viewpoint will invariably influence his "hearing," in spite of his sincerity and his honest attempts to be objective and open-minded. The third element refers to the methodology the researcher uses in the process of understanding and applying the concepts presented in the passage he investigates.

The purpose of this appendix is threefold: First, to find out whether Ellen White's writings really contain passages that advocate extreme ideas such as those presented by Elder Jones and his followers. Second, to explore some reasons why their views do not truly reflect the passages they claim for support, and to examine some of the methodological inadequacies that led them to their mistaken conclusions. And third, to establish as far as possible the true meaning and real intent some of the statements involved. In other words, we wish to show how such passages actually agree with the concepts we have established from Ellen White's writings in this book.

We have divided our discussion into two general sections. In the first one we considered some Ellen White statements that seem to endorse the idea, advanced by Jones and his supporters, that both man's body and his character must be fully restored to sinlessness and holiness before the end of probation. Unfortunately, space considerations do not allow us to treat this subject as thoroughly as desired. In the second section we examine in depth the one passage in Ellen White's writings that appears to provide the strongest

171

support to the theory that the believers who will be alive at the Second Advent must be sinlessly perfect like Jesus.

I. Ellen White's "Support" for the Idea That Believers Must Reach a State of Total Sanctification Before Probation Ends

The concepts advanced by E. R. Jones, the holy flesh people, and their followers (from now on referred to simply as the holy flesh doctrine) can be summarized as follows: 1. The believers who will be alive when Jesus returns can and must reach a state of flawless righteousness of being. The physical, moral, and spiritual aspects of their being—their body as well as their character— must be sinlessly perfect, just as Jesus is. 2. They must learn to live without sinning and to render flawless obedience to the will of God. 3. Finally, they must achieve this double objective fully before the world's probation comes to an end. Otherwise they disqualify themselves for salvation.

A-1. The Believer's Body Must Be Totally Sanctified Before the World's Probation Comes to an End

In this section we will use the issue of the reproduction of the image of God in the believer to illustrate how a faulty methodology can lead to the conclusion that Ellen White supports the idea that even the believer's body must regain original holiness during his present life on earth. In the process we will see how a faulty methodology results in extreme and unwarranted views even when most of the steps leading to the final conclusion are logical and valid. To begin, let us state four basic points that we can adequately establish from her writings:

172

APPENDIX

1. God created man in His own image, an image that included man's total person—the spiritual, moral, and physical dimensions of his being *(Education,* pp. 15, 20; *Patriarchs and Prophets,* p. 45; cf. *The Great Controversy,* p. 645). 2. The image of God in man has been marred and well-nigh obliterated by sin *(Patriarchs and Prophets,* p. 595; *Education,* p. 76; *Testimonies,* vol. 4, p. 294). 3. Christ came in order to restore the image of God in man *(The Desire of Ages,* pp. 37, 38, 478, 671; *Fundamentals of Christian Education,* p. 436; *The Great Controversy,* p. 645). 4. The restoration of God's image in man is made possible through such means as the work of the Holy Spirit, the knowledge of God, and obedience to the Ten Commandments *(The Desire of Ages,* p. 391; *Testimonies,* vol. 8, p. 289; *In Heavenly Places,* p. 146).

One can build an apparently strong case for the idea that the entire being of man—his spirit, soul, and body—has to be restored to holiness before the end of probation by quoting a carefully selected group of Ellen White passages such as the following ones:

> The sanctification set forth in the Sacred Scriptures has to do with *the entire being—spirit, soul, and body (The Sanctified Life,* p. 7; italics supplied). The true Christian obtains an experience which *brings holiness.* He is without a spot of guilt upon the conscience or a taint of corruption upon the soul. . . . His *body* is a fit temple for the Holy Spirit *(In Heavenly Places,* p. 200; italics supplied).

> Every Christian may enjoy the blessing of sanctifica-tion *(The Sanctified Life,* p. 85). Through obedience comes *sanctification of body,* soul, and spirit *(My Life Today,* p. 250). Everyone who by faith obeys God's commandments *will reach the condition of sinlessness in which Adam lived before his transgression (In Heavenly Places,* p. 146; italics supplied).

173

When the Lord comes, those who *are holy* will be holy still. Those who *have preserved their bodies and spirits in holiness, in sanctification and honor,* will then receive the finishing touch of immortality. . . . As we lay hold upon the truth of God, its influence affects us. It elevates us and *removes from us every imperfection and sin,* of whatever nature. Thus we are prepared to see the King in His beauty and finally to unite with the pure and heavenly angels in the kingdom of glory. *It is here that this work is to be accomplished for us, here that our bodies and spirits are to be fitted for immortality.* . . . And *what is the work that we are to undertake here* just previous to receiving immortality? It is *to preserve our bodies holy,* our spirits pure, that we may stand forth unstained amid the corruptions teeming around us in these last days *(Testimonies,* vol. 2, pp. 355, 356; italics supplied).

By placing the emphasis on certain aspects of these passages and pushing their literal wording to the limit, it is possible to draw a conclusion similar to this one: Christ came that the image of God may be reproduced in man. Through obedience comes sanctification of body, soul, and spirit, and everyone who obeys will reach the condition of sinlessness in which Adam lived. Since it is here—in this world—that our bodies and spirits are to be fitted for immortality, it follows that we have to reach such a state of total sanctification during our present lives before the end of probation.

It is important to note that such a concept has a considerable degree of internal consistency. According to the passages just quoted, *the whole image* of God is to be reflected in the believer, not just some of its parts. Therefore, *if God's image is to be restored during the present life at all, then the process must include both man's character and his body.* To leave the body out of the restorative process splits the image of God, and hence destroys the whole argument.

174

According to this view, the work of the Spirit and the believer's experiences in the present life are sufficient in themselves to complete the restorative process. That is why its proponents say that the last generation of believers will be able to reach the condition in which they will be worthy to earn God's final verdict of approval at the pre-Advent judgment on the basis of their personal accomplishments. God will not condemn them, because they no longer have anything wrong with them. He will accept them because the spiritual wholeness they achieved in their personal lives makes them worthy of His acceptance. The image of God—embracing both their personal character and their basic nature as human beings—has already been fully restored. As a result, they are perfectly righteous, like Jesus, and therefore worthy of eternal life.

A-2. An Examination of the Idea That Man's Body Must Be Restored to a State of Total Sanctification Before Probation Ends

It seems rather obvious that one can build as "good" a case and find as much Ellen White "support" for the idea that the body of man has to be restored to sinless perfection as for any other aspect of the holy flesh doctrine. Therefore, if the concept does indeed accurately represent what Ellen White taught, then the church should have had no difficulty accepting it as a truly Adventist position.

That has most definitely not been the case, however. Instead, we find this: 1. The Adventist Church has never endorsed the idea that the image of God—embracing the moral, spiritual, and physical dimensions of man's being—will be fully restored in the believer before the end of probation. 2. Although the literal reading of many passages in her writings appears to express ideas similar to what E. R. Jones, the holy flesh people, and their followers advocated, Ellen White rejected their views, rebuked them for misusing her writings in support of their beliefs, and warned the Adventist community about the dangers their teachings pose for the church at large.

These two factors alone should have kept us from ever entertaining such extreme ideas again. Unfortunately the history of our church indicates that while the holy flesh movement was short-lived, the peculiar mind-set its adherents exhibited, the extreme views they proposed, and the inadequate methodology they used in their interpretation of both Scripture and Ellen White's writings have remained with us. It seems that there always exists a segment of the Adventist Church that unmistakably resembles the former movement, that has a strong attraction to the idea of complete moral perfection and total holiness of being, and that has an exaggerated fascination with the prospect of reaching a state of sinlessness—being like Jesus—before the end of probation.

Since the Adventist Church has so categorically rejected the idea that God's image—comprising man's spirit, soul, and body—will be completely restored in the believer this side of glorification, we will limit our discussion to considering briefly just a few statements that should help us to reach a more balanced understanding of the issue.

> Much may be done to restore the moral image of God in man, to improve the physical, mental, and moral capabilities. . . . And while we cannot claim perfection of the flesh, we may have Christian perfection of the soul. Through the sacrifice made in our behalf, sins may be perfectly forgiven. Our dependence is not in what man can do; it is in what God can do for man through Christ.

When we surrender ourselves wholly to God, and fully believe, the blood of Christ cleanses from all sin *(Selected Messages,* book 2, p. 32).

Notice several points here: 1. *"Much may be done"* to restore God's image in man, to improve the moral, mental, and physical capabilities. Clearly it is a beginning, an improvement, but not a full restoration to the moral perfection and spiritual wholeness that God initially created.

2. *"We cannot claim perfection of the flesh."* Since the expression *the flesh* really refers to our basic nature as sinful human beings and not to our blood, tissues, and bones, this passage actually establishes the fact that we cannot claim perfection of what we are as beings, and not merely that we cannot perfect our physical bodies in this life.

3. *We may have perfection of the soul. "Through the sacrifice made in our behalf, sins may be perfectly forgiven."* Note that Ellen White does not link soul perfection to something that happens in the believer—such as his moral transformation, character development, and spiritual maturation. Nor does she attribute it to something the believer does—such as his flawless obedience and sinless living. Instead, she associates soul perfection with what God does for the believer through Christ, namely the perfect forgiveness and total cleansing that only the Saviour's atoning blood can produce.

The following passage is even clearer in its rejection of the idea that we can achieve perfection while in the flesh:

> If those who speak so freely of perfection in the flesh could see things in the true light, they would recoil with horror from their presumptuous ideas. . . . Let this phase of doctrine be carried a little further, and it will lead to the

claim that its advocates cannot sin; that since they have holy flesh, their actions are all holy *(ibid.).*

Three concepts here particularly relate to our topic: 1. Those who believe that it is possible for us to be perfect *in the flesh*—that is, in our present sinful condition as fallen beings—*do not see things in their true light.* 2. If they could view things as they really are, they would recoil with horror from *"their presumptuous ideas."* 3. The belief of perfection in the flesh leads to another error, namely *the mistaken idea that because they have become holy, they now can live without sinning.*

The third point radically contradicts a concept we discussed earlier, namely the idea that because our natures are fallen, sinful, and unholy, we are incapable of rendering perfect obedience. Notice:

> It was possible for Adam, before the fall, to form a righteous character by obedience to God's law. But he failed to do this, and because of his sin our natures are fallen and we cannot make ourselves righteous. Since we are sinful, unholy, we cannot perfectly obey the holy law. We have no righteousness of our own with which to meet the claims of the law of God *(Steps to Christ,* p. 62). The law demands righteousness, and this the sinner owes to the law; but he is incapable of rendering it *(Selected Messages,* book 1, p. 367). [The law] could not justify man, because in his sinful nature he could not keep the law *(Patriarchs and Prophets,* p. 373).

The perfection theology we are discussing has at least three major negative side effects: First, after endeavoring for a time to become perfect in character and behavior, many become discouraged and often give up Christianity altogether. It is particularly true of young people who as a rule are too honest to deceive themselves into believing that they are indeed becoming sinlessly perfect like Jesus. Second, the belief in sinless perfection appears to have little—if any—positive effect on the lives of those who embrace it. One observes no perceptible evidence that they are better parents, neighbors, or workers, or that the fruit of the Spirit—such as love, kindness, tolerance, and faith—has reached a level of greater maturity in them than in the rest of Christ's imperfect but growing disciples.

Two basic reasons account for this: 1. Those enticed by such ideas develop an obsession with holiness that is strictly theological or intellectual. They seem to think that what really counts is not tangible evidence that they are indeed changing, growing, and maturing as Christians, but proof that they have endorsed the idea that sinless perfection is possible in this life. They assume that if they just hold on to their belief, they will somehow be part of the remnant. Consequently, they usually are more concerned with convincing others about the correctness of their theories than with endeavoring to develop the fruit of the Spirit in their personal lives.

2. The eschatological nature of the perfection doctrine offers its adherents hope for tomorrow without imposing any obligations for today. By projecting the attainment of perfection into the future, it distracts them from the opportunities and responsibilities of the present. Thus, instead of motivating them to strive for progressive victory over specific problem areas in their lives now, it deludes them with the unrealistic hope of total victory right before probation ends.

The third negative side effect of the belief that we can be sinlessly perfect in this life is its tremendous capacity to beguile those who embrace it, making it extremely difficult either to dissuade them of their mistaken ideas or to lead them to a more balanced understanding of the gospel of Christ. Ellen White knew the problem from personal experience:

> We feel sad to see professed Christians led astray by the false and bewitching theory that they are perfect, because it is so difficult to undeceive them and lead them into the right path *(The Sanctified Life,* p. 12). Self-righteousness is the danger of this age; it separates the soul from Christ. Those who trust in their own righteousness cannot understand how salvation comes through Christ *(Faith and Works,* p. 96).

Notice the following points: 1. Those who believe they are perfect—who trust in their own merits for a right standing with God—have been led astray by an erroneous and seductive idea. 2. Therefore, it is difficult to break its hold on them and help them understand how salvation comes through Christ. 3. Ellen White expressed sadness and pain at finding them so entrenched in their deceptive theory that they were no longer able to understand, and unwilling to accept, the gospel.

It is important to remember that a person does not need to actually say, "I am perfect," in order to be guilty of the arrogant attitude Ellen White found so offensive. If such were the case, then her statements would apply to few people, since no one in his right mind ever dares to make such a claim. Instead, she contradicted a particular kind of theology, a specific viewpoint, namely the false and bewitching theory that sinless perfection must become a reality to us during our present lives.

A-3. A More Balanced View on the Issue of the Reproduction of the Image of God in the Believer

To conclude our discussion in this section, we will state what we consider to be a more balanced understanding of this concept—an understanding that fully harmonizes with the theological scenario, based on Ellen White's writings, that we have described in this book: The image of God begins to be restored in the believer the moment he is spiritually united to Christ at conversion, continues to be more fully reproduced in him throughout his life as a Christian, and reaches its complete, final, and permanent restoration at the second coming of Christ. At that time—when the kingdom of glory replaces the kingdom of grace—God will return all the redeemed to the condition of perfect spiritual wholeness with which He created man in the beginning. As a result of His re-creative act, all the redeemed will then—for the first time ever—reflect the image of God in their own person as fully as did Adam and Eve before the Fall.

According to this view, the work of the Holy Spirit and the believer's experiences in the present life—his change, growth, and maturation—begin the work of transformation, but only God's re-creative act at the time of glorification will complete Christ's image in the redeemed. Since full restoration is possible only at the Second Coming, the last generation of believers will be as dependent on the mediation of Christ in the Father's presence as were all previous ones. In spite of their progress in spiritual growth and moral development, the last generation will not find acceptance with God on the basis of who they are or what they did, but on the fact that they come to the Father through the Son, and therefore are righteous in Christ.

B-1. The Believer's Character Must Reach a State of Sinless Perfection Before the End of Probation

Since the idea that the believer has the entire image of God—spirit, soul, and body—reconstituted in him before the end of probation is indefensible, some have argued that it is only the believer's character that must reach a state of sinless perfection by that time. The following are some of the passages they use as support:

Whatever may be our inherited or cultivated tendencies to wrong, we can overcome through the power that He is ready to impart *(The Ministry of Healing,* p. 176; italics supplied). There is *no difficulty* within or without that cannot be surmounted in His strength. . . . There is *no nature* so rebellious that Christ cannot subdue it, *no temper* so stormy that He cannot quell it, if the heart is surrendered to His keeping (Ellen G. White, in *The Watchman,* Apr. 28, 1908; italics supplied).

Through the plan of redemption, God has provided means for *subduing every sinful trait,* and *resisting every temptation,* however strong *(Selected Messages,* book 1, p. 82; italics supplied). We can overcome. Yes; fully, entirely. Jesus died to make a way of escape for us, that we might *overcome every evil temper, every sin, every temptation,* and sit down at last with Him *(Testimonies,* vol. 1, p. 144; italics supplied). Those who, through an intelligent understanding of the Scriptures, view the cross aright, those who truly believe in Jesus, have a sure foundation for their faith. They have that faith which works by love and *purifies the soul from all its hereditary and cultivated imperfections (ibid.,* vol. 6, p. 238; italics supplied).

God expects us to build characters in accordance with the pattern set before us. We are to lay brick by brick, adding grace to grace, finding our weak points and correcting them in accordance with the directions given *(Child Guidance,* p. 165). Through affliction God reveals to us the plague spots in our characters, that by His grace we may overcome our faults *(The Desire of Ages,* p. 301). Trial is part of the education given in the school of Christ, to purify God's children from the dross of earthliness. . . .

Often He permits the fires of affliction to burn, that they may be purified *(The Acts of the Apostles,* p. 524).

On the basis of a literal reading of such statements, some argue for complete sanctification and flawless perfection something like this: 1. We can surmount all our inherited and cultivated tendencies to evil through the means God has provided. 2. Trials and afflictions are God's instruments to reveal to us our character defects so that we may correct them. 3. A right understanding of Scripture and true faith in Jesus purify the soul of all its imperfections. 4. God has provided the means for resisting every temptation, however strong, so that we may overcome fully, entirely. 5. Therefore, nothing could possibly hinder the last generation of believers from reaching a state of total righteousness of being and of entire sinlessness of conduct.

B-2. An Examination of the Idea That the Believer's Character Must Reach a State of Sinless Perfection Before Probation Ends

Before we draw any conclusions either about the precise meaning of the passages just quoted or about Ellen White's true position on the subject, we must consider some factors and concepts essential to a correct understanding of the whole issue: 1. There is nothing intrinsically wrong with these statements—she could hardly have worded them otherwise. Ellen White could not have said, for example, that we can overcome only *some* evil tendencies to evil, that Jesus can subdue only *some* rebellious natures and quell only *some* stormy tempers. Besides not being the whole truth, such phrasing would lead to either rationalizations or discouragement on the part of readers struggling with such things in their lives.

2. The problem is created when we push the pas-

sages beyond their proper limits, when we respect their wording but not their intent, or when we make their literal meaning neutralize the deeper, more significant concepts they contain. There is a radical difference between saying, for example, that God often uses trial and affliction to reveal to us some specific defects in our characters and claiming that trial and affliction are the means by which we will overcome *each and every one* of our imperfections, so that we may achieve flawless perfection. We have no more right to claim that we can be sinlessly perfect because Ellen White says we can overcome *every* sin than to claim that we can have an infallible theology because Jesus promised that the Holy Spirit "will guide you into *all* truth" (John 16:13), or that we can predict the future because Paul said we "can do *all* things through Christ" (Phil. 4:13, KJV).

To illustrate how a reader aided by a faulty methodology can be led into theological pitfalls, let us suppose that Brother A and Brother B read the passages we quoted in section B-1. Brother A is experiencing some difficult spiritual problems. He wrestles with some deep-seated tendencies to evil, struggles with his stormy temper, and faces some persistent temptations in his personal life. Brother B, on the other hand, looks for Ellen White support for the idea that the last generation of believers must overcome all forms of sin in their lives and develop flawless perfection of being before the world's probation ends.

Obviously, each man will interpret and apply the concepts expressed in the passages in a radically different way from the other. What each "sees" in them, what they mean to each one personally, may be poles apart. Brother A will probably realize from them that none of us has a sin problem so unique, severe, or complicated that God cannot help us solve it. He will see that his case is not hopeless after all—as he felt tempted to believe. And he will take courage in the assurance that, serious though his problem might be, God has provided the means by which he will eventually find a solution.

In contrast, Brother B will most likely use such quotations as evidence that Ellen White's writings support his extreme ideas. After all, if there is nothing that cannot be overcome through the means God has provided, what could possibly keep the last generation of believers from becoming as sinlessnessly perfect and as morally righteous as Jesus Himself?

It is at this precise point that a faulty methodology gets us into problems. In order to be true to the text, Brother B must allow Ellen White to speak for herself. He must begin his study by establishing as precisely as possible what exactly it was that she meant when she first wrote these passages. Thus, he has to determine whether she was trying to prove—as he is—that the believer can and must reach a state of sinless perfection before probation ends. If that was not what she intended to prove, then Brother B has no right to use her statements in support of his ideas. To do so would distort her teachings, and hence would be both ethically wrong and theologically misleading.

Unless Brother B interprets these passages within the thematic context to which they belong, he will place a different construction on what they actually say and consequently make them mean something radically different from what Ellen White had in mind. As a result, the concepts she attempted to express and the ideas Brother B advocates will be unrelated, in spite of the similarity in language used. A passage that is valid and proper when interpreted and applied as the author intended it to be can lead into serious theological difficulties when we disregard either its boundaries, its intent, or its deeper meaning.

3. Although Christ's atoning death took place at a specific time in history, His redemptive work—with all the wonderful possibilities it opens before the believer—embraces all mankind from the beginning to the end of time. Thus all God's redemptive promises apply with equal force to the very first sinner who turned to God in repentance and faith and to the very last one who responds right before probation ends.

Therefore, the assurance of victory given in passages such as those we are considering here is not something new and different that was not real before but became a possibility at the time Ellen White wrote about it. Much less is it a special promise that applies only to the last generation of believers as they prepare for the pre-Advent judgment, the end of probation, and the time of trouble. On the contrary, her statements extend to all believers of all generations, and therefore we should not treat them as though they were either a particular obligation or an exclusive privilege of the last generation.

This leads us to some crucial questions: If obtaining the victory over everything that must be overcome in order to achieve sinless perfection were as simple as the passages quoted in section B-1 seem to indicate, why is it that no one has ever transcended his personal sinfulness, imperfection, and unworthiness? Why has no one ever outgrown his fallen condition and succeeded in rendering flawless obedience? Why did not even the prophets and apostles, those spiritual giants who lived closest to God—many of whom died for their faith—ever reach a state of total sanctification and complete personal righteousness? Notice:

APPENDIX

None of the apostles and prophets ever claimed to be without sin. Men who have lived the nearest to God, men who would sacrifice life itself rather than knowingly commit a wrong act, men whom God has honored with divine light and power, have confessed the sinfulness of their nature. They have put no confidence in the flesh, have claimed no righteousness of their own, but have trusted wholly in the righteousness of Christ *(The Acts of the Apostles,* p. 561).

When the Spirit of Christ stirs the heart with its marvelous awakening power, there is a sense of deficiency in the soul that leads to contrition of mind, and humiliation of self, rather than to proud boasting of what has been acquired (Ellen G. White, in *Review and Herald,* Oct. 16, 1888). No man can look within himself and find anything in his character that will recommend him to God, or make his acceptance sure. . . . Jesus alone is our Redeemer, our Advocate and Mediator; in Him is our only hope for pardon, peace, and righteousness *(Selected Messages,* book 1, pp. 332, 333).

Since we already discussed this issue earlier, we will provide just five basic reasons that should help to answer our questions adequately enough for our purpose here:

One: The formation of a righteous character is a progressive activity that *lasts a lifetime.*

Character building is the work, not of a day, nor of a year, but of a lifetime. *The struggle for conquest over self, for holiness and heaven, is a lifelong struggle.* Without continual effort and constant activity, there can be no advancement in the divine life, no attainment of the victor's crown *(The Ministry of Healing,* p. 452; italics supplied).

The formation of a noble character is the work of a lifetime and must be the result of diligent and persevering effort. God gives opportunities; success depends upon the use made of them *(Patriarchs and Prophets,* p. 223). The precious graces of the Holy Spirit are not developed in a moment. Courage, fortitude, meekness, faith, unwavering trust in God's power to save, are acquired by *the experience of years (Testimonies,* vol. 8, p. 314; italics supplied).

On the basis of these passages, we conclude: 1. Only those who begin forming noble characters at birth and successfully continue doing so throughout their entire lifetime stand a chance at developing a flawless character. 2. Since it takes an entire life span to form a righteous character, it follows that a person does not complete it before he reaches the end of his days. 3. Because the close of probation does not complete anything, but interrupts everything, it also halts the process of character development, thus frustrating the possibilities of its completion.

Two: A righteous character can be formed *only through perfect obedience.*

True sanctification . . . consists in the cheerful performance of daily duties *in perfect obedience* to the will of God *(Christ's Object Lessons,* p. 360; italics supplied). It was possible for Adam, before the fall, to form a righteous character by obedience to God's law. But he failed to do this, and because of his sin our natures are fallen and we cannot make ourselves righteous. Since we are sinful, unholy, *we cannot perfectly obey* the holy law. We have no righteousness of our own with which to meet the claims of the law of God *(Steps to Christ,* p. 62; italics supplied).

Because righteous characters can be developed only through perfect obedience, and our obedience is at best partial and imperfect, it logically follows that we cannot form characters of such quality that God can accept them on their own merits.

APPENDIX

When we combine points one and two, we find that *only those who rendered perfect obedience all their lives—from birth to death—could possibly achieve righteous characters.* This leaves Jesus in a category all by Himself, and rightly so, since He is the only one who ever lived in full harmony with God's will in all respects throughout His life. But those who belong to one of the following groups lack the qualifications that would enable them to develop righteous characters:

1. Those who experience periods of stagnation or regression at some time during their lifetime. Their temporary failure to grow and mature delays their progress and thus frustrates their chances at completing their character development before the end of their lives. 2. Those whose lives are cut short by premature death—through accident, sickness, war, etc.—and hence have a reduced period of time during which to outgrow their imperfection and thus achieve sinless righteousness. 3. Those who accept the gospel late in life and consequently do not have a full lifetime during which to overcome their sinful attitudes, tendencies, and habits, and to replace them with righteous ones. It is particularly true with those who experience conversion for the first time shortly before the end of probation. Since "the precious graces of the Holy Spirit" "are acquired by the experience of years" and they have but a short period of time during which to acquire such virtues, one must assume that they are automatically disqualified.

Evidently we have a double problem here. On the one hand, it is difficult to understand how anyone could advance the idea that the millions of believers living on earth during the time of the end will all complete the formation of mature Christian characters right before probation ends. Like any other generation, this one will consist of individuals differing in background, in personal characteristics, and in spiritual experience. There will be small children, inexperienced teenagers, sickly and weakened older persons. Some believers will be seasoned Christians, while others will be newly born babes in Christ. Since each of them will have a unique experience with God and find himself at a stage of change, growth, and maturation that is different from others, it is totally unrealistic to expect that all of them will achieve character perfection all at the same time.

On the other hand, it is difficult to understand how one could possibly confuse such theories with the scriptural gospel. We saw earlier that, according to Scripture, all who accept Christ's redemptive work on their behalf will have eternal life. Jesus "is able to save completely those who come to God through him" (Heb. 7:25) regardless of their race, color, geographical location, the particular time when they lived, or the specific point during their life span when they responded to the gospel in repentance and faith. Further, we saw that *all God's sons and daughters in Christ are heirs to the kingdom, not just those adopted early enough in life to have sufficient time to presumably complete the process of overcoming their defects, developing righteous characters, and learning to live without sinning.*

Because he turned to Jesus at the eleventh hour, the thief on the cross experienced hardly any character development or behavior modification before he sealed his eternal destiny at death. Yet Jesus promised that he will be in paradise. Obviously such a "burning stick snatched from the fire" (Zech. 3:2) is not an isolated case. Only God knows how many millions throughout human history have turned to God for the first time on their deathbeds. Likewise, only He knows how many millions more will for the first time ever accept the gospel in response to the outpouring of the latter rain of the Holy Spirit shortly before the end of time.

Now, if only those who outgrew all their imperfections, developed flawless righteousness of being, and learned to live without sinning were safe to be saved, then none of the millions of last-minute believers would have any hope of eternal life. In that case, all those who accepted God's saving grace shortly before they died, and all those who will become believers in response to God's final appeal right before probation ends, will be eternally lost because they did not have the time required to develop perfection of character. Such an outcome would mean that the scriptural promises of forgiveness and reconciliation to those who come to the Father through the Son do not apply to them; that they yield to the Spirit's moving, accept God's last message of mercy and place their trust fully in Christ's redemptive work on their behalf in vain. A theory that creates complications like these is clearly out of harmony with the gospel of Scripture.

Three: In passages like the ones we quoted in section B-1, in which Ellen White encourages the believers to continue their Christian warfare and urges them to reach for a higher goal and to strive toward perfection, she is positive about their possibilities of success. However, in passages in which she describes the experience of those who died in Christ and those who will face the pre-Advent judgment during their lifetime, she presents a radically different picture. As we saw earlier (in the third and fourth chapters), she clearly indicates that neither those who were still living by faith when they died nor those who are living by faith when probation ends reached or reach the goal of sinless perfection. In both cases she specifically mentions their "defects of character" or "defective characters" and

191

their "unlikeness to Christ," and points out the fact that they are declared righteous before God strictly *on the basis of the Saviour's merits* imputed to them by faith.

Four: Ellen White's writings portray character perfection as *relative and progressive,* not total and complete.

> The germination of the seed represents the beginning of spiritual life, and the development of the plant is a figure of the development of character. There can be no life without growth. . . . *At every stage of development our life may be perfect;* yet if God's purpose for us is fulfilled, there will be constant advancement *(Education,* pp. 105, 106; italics supplied). *We are not yet perfect;* but it is our privilege to cut away from the entanglements of self and sin, and *advance to perfection (The Acts of the Apostles,* p. 565; italics supplied).

> Man may grow up into Christ, his living head. It is not the work of a moment, but that of a lifetime. By growing daily in the divine life, *he will not attain to the full stature of a perfect man in Christ until his probation ceases.* The growing is a continuous work *(Testimonies,* vol. 4, p. 367; italics supplied). So long as Satan reigns, we shall have self to subdue, besetting sins to overcome; *so long as life shall last, there will be no stopping place, no point which we can reach and say, I have fully attained (The Acts of the Apostles,* pp. 560, 561; italics supplied). In ourselves *we are sinners;* but in Christ we are righteous *(Selected Messages,* book 1, p. 394; italics supplied).

> Those who are really seeking to perfect Christian character *will never indulge the thought that they are sinless.* . . . The nearer they approach to [Christ's] divine image, the more clearly will they discern its spotless perfection, and the more deeply will they feel *their own defects (The Sanctified Life,* p. 7; italics supplied). There can be no self-exaltation, *no boastful claim to freedom from sin,* on the part of those who walk in the shadow of Calvary's cross.

APPENDIX

... Those who live nearest to Jesus discern most clearly *the frailty and sinfulness of humanity,* and their only hope is in the merit of a crucified and risen Saviour *(The Great Controversy,* p. 471; italics supplied).

If we are to understand Ellen White's complex view on this topic, we must give adequate attention to several points here: 1. Although she says our lives are "perfect," yet at the same time she tells us that "we are not yet perfect." We have defects, we are sinful, we fall short of the mark, and we are unworthy. 2. While our lives may be "perfect" at every stage of development—as a recently germinated seed, as a growing plant, as a flowering bush—we still continue to advance toward perfection. 3. Our battle with self and sin, on the one hand, and our striving for righteousness and holiness, on the other, will never be complete in this life. We will never reach the place where we are free from sin or fully attain to character perfection before our probation ends.

In view of these factors, we conclude that when Ellen White speaks of the believer's character perfection, she means something radically different from the ideas advanced by E. R. Jones, the holy flesh people, and others. Jones and his group speak about a finalized product—a state or plateau of absolute sinlessness and total righteousness that the believer actually reaches. They write of characters without any flaws, shortcomings, or deficiencies—characters that have the same moral quality and spiritual perfection as the Saviour's. Should those who supposedly possess such characters closely behold the character of Christ, they would not realize their own defects, as Ellen White says is the case with all true believers. Instead, they would conclude that they have indeed equaled the absolute pattern that Christ's character establishes, and hence are worthy of eternal life.

Ellen White, on the other hand, tells of a process of change, growth, and maturation that is progressive and will never reach its culmination in our present lives. She describes an experience possible only through our faith relationship with Jesus Christ, and that takes place within the context of the covenant of grace. It brings us into gradual spiritual unity with Christ, and makes us increasingly aware of our total dependence on His saving righteousness, imputed to us by faith, for a right standing with God. According to her view, our personal relationship with Christ is the dynamic reality that causes both our acceptance with God and our growth as disciples.

Five: Ellen White's writings center the believer's perfection of character in Christ and His redemptive work on man's behalf.

> Jesus came to restore in man the image of his Maker. *None but Christ can fashion anew the character* that has been ruined by sin. . . . He came to lift us up from the dust, to reshape the marred character after the pattern of His divine character, and *to make it beautiful with His own glory* (*The Desire of Ages,* pp. 37, 38; italics supplied).

> Through the merits of Christ, *through His righteousness, which by faith is imputed unto us, we are to attain to the perfection of Christian character* (*Testimonies,* vol. 5, p. 744; italics supplied). Though the moral image of God was almost obliterated by the sin of Adam, through the merits and power of Jesus it may be renewed. *Man may stand with the moral image of God in his character; for Jesus will give it to him* (Ellen G. White, in *Review and Herald,* June 10, 1890; italics supplied).

APPENDIX

Those who reject *the gift of Christ's righteousness* are rejecting *the attributes of character* which would constitute them the sons and daughters of God. They are rejecting *that which alone could give them a fitness for a place at the marriage feast (Christ's Object Lessons,* pp. 316, 317; italics supplied).

We must catch several points that she makes. 1. Ellen White identifies the work of restoring God's image and reshaping our characters as Christ's, not ours. 2. He will make our character beautiful "with His own glory"—clearly something He provides and not something we develop. 3. We are to attain to the perfection of Christian character through the merits and righteousness of Christ imputed to us by faith. It means that the method or way for attaining character perfection does not center on our personal growth, but on Christ's mediation in our behalf.

4. The believer will again have God's image in his character because *"Jesus will give it to him."* 5. Christ's righteousness, which can be ours only as a gift, constitutes "the attributes of character" that alone can make us fit for the kingdom. 6. The character Christ formed as God/man, He will impute to us, and it is our possession of Christ's character that determines our acceptance with God.

As we have clearer views of Christ's spotless and infinite purity we shall feel as did Daniel when he beheld the glory of the Lord and said, "My comeliness was turned in me into corruption" (Dan. 10:8). We cannot say, "I am sinless," till this vile body is changed and fashioned like unto His glorious body. But if we constantly seek to follow Jesus, the blessed hope is ours of standing before the throne of God without spot, or wrinkle, or any such thing, complete in Christ, robed in His righteousness and perfection *(That I May Know Him,* p. 361).

The preceding passage reinforces two points we have mentioned earlier: 1. *We cannot claim sinlessness until the Second Advent,* at which time God will restore us to humanity's original state of sinless perfection. As we pointed out before, the reason we cannot claim sinlessness is not that there is something wrong with the actual utterance of the words, but because it is not true. 2. If we constantly seek to follow Jesus, *we will stand before the throne of God complete in Christ, robed in His righteousness and perfection.* Clearly, what enables us to appear flawless before God is not the perfection of character we have actually developed, but the righteousness of Christ that He imputes to us by faith.

The following passage provides the balance needed to understand this concept correctly. Speaking about Daniel's experience in the presence of the Son of God (Dan. 10:5-8), Ellen White states:

> *All who are truly sanctified* will have a similar experience. The clearer their views of the greatness, glory, and perfection of Christ, the more vividly will they *see their own weakness and imperfection.* They will have *no disposition to claim a sinless character;* that which has appeared right and comely in themselves will, in contrast with Christ's purity and glory, appear only as unworthy and corruptible. It is when men . . . have very indistinct views of Christ that they say, "I am sinless; I am sanctified" *(The Sanctified Life,* pp. 50, 51; italics supplied).

Notice: 1. This passage does not describe the condition either of new believers or of those who have a precarious spiritual life. Instead, it describes those who, like Daniel, "are truly sanctified." 2. Such believers do not consider themselves as weak, imperfect, and unworthy because they lack spiritual discernment, but because they have a reliable view of the perfection of Christ. *It is in contrast to His purity that they see themselves as they really are*—as God would view them if Christ's perfect righteousness did not cover them.

3. Finally, these believers do not refrain from asserting that they have sinless characters either because extreme modesty or because making such a claim is inherently wrong—after all, there is nothing wrong with stating something that is true to fact, something that one can substantiate with solid evidence. The reason they "have no disposition to claim a sinless character" is that their distinct view of Christ has made them painfully aware that their characters really are far from being perfect and *therefore* it would be wrong for them to make such a statement.

> Christ presents before us the highest perfection of Christian character, which *throughout our lifetime we should aim to reach.* . . . Concerning this perfection Paul writes: "Not as though I had already attained, either were already perfect: but *I follow after.* . . . I press toward the mark for the prize of the high calling of God in Christ Jesus" (Phil 3:12-14) *(That I May Know Him,* p. 130; italics supplied).

> The ideal of Christian character is Christlikeness. There is opened before us a path of *constant advancement.* We have an object to gain, a standard to reach, that includes everything good and pure and noble and elevated. There should be *continual striving and constant progress* onward and upward toward perfection of character *(Testimonies,* vol. 8, p. 64; italics supplied). When it is in the heart to obey God, when efforts are put forth to this end, Jesus accepts this disposition and effort as man's best service, and *He makes up for the deficiency with His own divine merit (My Life Today,* p. 250; italics supplied).

These passages bring together the three most significant elements concerning the issue of character development: 1. The standard that has been set—the ideal toward which we must strive—is Christlikeness. It includes everything good and pure and noble and elevated. 2. The believer's duty is to strive, to press on, to aim for the attainment of the goal of character perfection, to experience constant progress onward and upward throughout his life. 3. When that is the believer's deliberate objective—when he does what God knows is reasonable to expect of him—then Jesus accepts his disposition and efforts and makes up for his deficiencies. As a result, the believer is accepted as being righteous in Christ, by faith, in spite of the fact that he is still imperfect and unworthy in himself, by nature.

B-3. A More Balanced Understanding of the Subject of Character Perfection

In general terms we can say that God wants to accomplish a double purpose through the plan of redemption: (1) to restore man to the condition of perfect spiritual wholeness in which He initially created him, and (2) to restore the relationship between Himself and man that sin broke. Such a dual restoration will enable the redeemed to be brought back into God's immediate presence to renew the spiritual unity and personal fellowship with God that Adam and Eve enjoyed before the Fall.

In most cases, God's plan for bringing man to his original state comes to full realization in three basic stages. 1. At conversion the sinner-turned-believer experiences a fundamental spiritual reawakening. His basic attitude toward God, himself, sin, and his fellowman changes radically. As his affections find a new center, his will becomes aligned with God's will and his life takes an entirely new direction.

2. Throughout his life as an adopted child of God in Christ he experiences a progressive change, growth,

and maturation that enables him to increasingly reflect the virtues of Christ's holy character in his personal life. This is a progressive work that varies from one person to another and is never fully completed in this life. During this time, "Christ works within us, and His righteousness is upon us" *(Selected Messages,* book 1, p. 360). Since what Jesus accomplishes within us involves what we are as sinful beings, it is always partial and incomplete, and therefore dependent upon His imputed merits for acceptance with God. In contrast, what He does for us involves what Christ is—His personal righteousness and perfect character—and therefore is always total, complete and fully acceptable to God on our behalf.

3. At the second coming of Christ, when the eternal replaces the temporal and incorruption the corruptible, all God's children will fully and permanently acquire a state of sinless perfection. Then, and not before, will God's plan for the redemption of man achieve its completion. Both the relationships sin destroyed and the beings it perverted will again be exactly what they were before the Fall.

II. A Significant and Controverted Passage Reexamined.

In this section we will illustrate how a careful investigation of a particular passage sometimes leads the researcher to an interpretation radically different from the conclusion he would have reached on the basis of a superficial reading of the text. We have chosen this particular passage for three basic reasons. First, it appears to support the theory that those believers alive at the Second Advent must be sinlessly perfect like Jesus. Second, it is part of a book first published in the 1880s, and therefore could have been one of the passages E. R. Jones and his followers used to bolster their extreme ideas. And third, it is not a personal testimony addressed to a particular individual but part of a book intended for wide public circulation—a fact that increases its theological significance.

> *Now, while our great High Priest is making the atonement for us, we should seek to become perfect in Christ.* Not even *by a thought* could our Saviour be brought to yield to the power of temptation. Satan finds in human hearts some point where he can gain a foothold; some sinful desire *is cherished,* by means of which his temptations assert their power. But Christ declared of Himself: "The prince of this world cometh, and hath nothing in me" (John 14:30). Satan could find nothing in the Son of God that would enable him to gain the victory. He had kept His Father's commandments, and there was no sin in Him that Satan could use to his advantage. *This is the condition in which those must be found who shall stand in the time of trouble (The Great Controversy,* p. 623; italics supplied).

A casual reading could easily lead to the impression that Ellen White agreed with the idea that before probation ends, God's people must develop a personal righteousness that measures up to that of Christ and learn to live without sinning—even by a thought—just as Jesus did. After all, the passage states that God's people have to be perfect, that Jesus didn't yield to temptation even by a thought, that Satan could find in Him no sin he could use to his advantage, and that this is the condition of those who shall endure the time of trouble.

However, upon closer investigation, we conclude that such an interpretation is unacceptable. First, because it creates some serious problems. Let us consider just three of them. 1. If Ellen White really believed that God's people can and must reach a state of sinless perfection—just like Jesus—before probation ends, then it is extremely difficult to understand why she opposed Jones so decisively when he promoted that idea. It is also hard to see how she could have advocated the very same teachings she called a deception, man-made tests, a message of error that prevents God's true message from being accepted, etc. Such a course of action would have been totally inconsistent—an obvious and unacceptable contradiction that would have severely damaged her credibility with those who want to take her seriously.

2. To make the passage endorse the ideas of Jones puts it in tension with its conceptual context. As we saw earlier, the chapter it is a part of establishes that God's people living through the time of trouble are no more sinless, righteous, or worthy of salvation than any previous generation of believers. She states that they can see little good in their entire lives and are fully conscious of their imperfection, weakness, and unworthiness, and, consequently, depend on Christ for a right standing with God. They have the assurance of eternal life, not because they transcended their lost condition and achieve total spiritual wholeness like Jesus, but because they have repented of their sin and accept fully Christ's redemptive work on their behalf.

3. If the quote really states that those who will stand in the time of trouble must be just as sinless and as righteous as Jesus, then it contradicts a considerable number of significant concepts clearly established elsewhere in Ellen White's writings. In that case, her writings would provide no help for the clarification of the dynamics of God's plan for the salvation of sinful man. On the contrary, by advocating two opposing views simultaneously, they would confuse and mislead the reader since the particular set of writings he happened to consult first would determine his conclusions. An

interpretation that leads to such significant problems has to be dismissed as inadequate.

The second reason the above interpretation is unacceptable is that it does not reflect the real meaning and true intent of the passage in question. As we examine it closely, we find that it contains four major concepts that we must consider in order to understand it correctly: 1. "*. . . we should seek to become perfect in Christ.*" There is a subtle yet extremely significant difference between desiring to "become perfect *in* Christ" and trying to be perfect *like* Christ. To be perfect *like* Christ is to be just as righteous, holy, and worthy in ourselves as Jesus was in Himself. It means achieving in our own lives a spiritual wholeness equal to the Saviour's perfection in every single respect. But that is not the goal this passage sets before the believer. Instead, it challenges the believer to become perfect *in* Christ, which, as we saw earlier—particularly in the first chapter—means to be righteous through the merits of Christ imputed to us by faith.

2. "*Now, while our great High Priest is making the atonement for us,* we should seek to become perfect in Christ." Two reasons compel us to become perfect in Christ now, while Jesus is still making atonement for us—why "those who delay a preparation for the day of God cannot obtain it in the time of trouble or at any subsequent time. The case of all such is hopeless" (*ibid.*, p. 620). First, because God's forgiveness for our sin and Christ's saving righteousness by means of which we are acceptable to God are mediated only through Christ while He actively ministers on our behalf in the Father's presence. It therefore follows that if we want our sins to go beforehand to judgment and be blotted out, if we want to be covered by the imputed righteousness of Christ and thus stand flawless before the tribunal of

God, then we must secure God's forgiveness and avail ourselves of the Saviour's merits before Jesus ceases to mediate on our behalf.

Second, because our eternal destiny will be sealed forever at that point in time when Jesus completes His mediatorial ministry by securing God's final and irreversible verdict of acceptance. Once the judgment ceases and our cases are permanently closed, it will be too late to do anything to change God's decision. Now we are on probation—now is the day of salvation. Therefore, whatever we intend to do to affect our eternal destiny one way or the other we must do now. The case of those who fail to become perfect in Christ now while He mediates in our behalf "is hopeless" precisely because once Jesus completes His mediatorial ministry in heaven, *the benefits of His redemptive work are no longer available to them.* As a result, they have lost the only means by which they can be reconciled to God and be adopted into His family of believers.

3. "Not even *by a thought* could our Saviour be brought to yield to the power of temptation." Since a thought is a conscious process, it follows that the passage describes Christ's response to situations He recognized as enticements to sin. *To yield even by a thought to a perceived temptation would have been to sin knowingly, deliberately, willfully.* So when Ellen White later states that "this is the condition in which those must be found who shall stand in the time of trouble," she does not say they have to develop in their personal lives a righteousness that measures up to the absolute perfection of Christ in all respects. Instead, the passage says that they must come to the place where they no longer yield to recognized temptation—where they *refuse to sin willfully.*

4. "Satan finds in the human hearts some point where he can gain a foothold; *some sinful desire is cherished*

. . ." Clearly the passage does not deal with sin in its broadest scope, but only with cherished sin. Ellen White here establishes a significant contrast between Jesus and the rest of us. *In the human heart Satan does find a foothold "by means of which his temptations assert their power."* Cherished sinful desires are like an open door that gives Satan access to the heart. They increase the power of his temptations and facilitate his victory over us. In contrast,

> *Satan could find nothing in the Son of God* that would enable him to gain the victory. He had kept His Father's commandments, and *there was no sin in Him that Satan could use to his advantage.*

We can thus see that what the quotation is really saying is that those who will stand in the time of trouble must reach "the condition" of having no cherished sinful desires which Satan could use to his advantage in his endeavor to cause their eternal ruin. The following passage helps us understand their experience:

> When we are clothed with the righteousness of Christ, we shall have no relish for sin; for Christ will be working with us. We may make mistakes, but we will hate the sin that caused the sufferings of the Son of God (Ellen G. White, in *Review and Herald,* Mar. 18, 1890).

On the basis of such considerations we conclude that this passage from Ellen White's writings indicates that those who shall endure through the time of trouble must have the following three characteristics: First, *they are perfect in Christ.* They are totally forgiven—cleansed in the atoning blood of Christ—and covered by the Saviour's imputed merits by virtue of which they stand before the Father righteous in Christ, by faith. Second, *they do not sin knowingly,* deliberately, willfully. And third, *they do not cherish any sinful desires* by means of which Satan could gain victory over them.

It is important to note that *the requirements described here represent neither a higher standard than what God has demanded in the past nor a new method for securing God's approval and being found worthy of eternal life.* At least four basic concepts discussed earlier bear this out: 1. God has always required perfect righteousness of being and total flawlessness of conduct from His children. So instead of introducing a new standard unique to the last generation of believers, Ellen White reaffirms God's existing requirement by establishing the fact that He will not lower His expectations for those "who shall stand in the time of trouble."

2. The only way for any fallen being to achieve either perfect righteousness of being or total flawlessness of conduct has always been through the imputed righteousness of Christ. The last generation will find acceptance with God in exactly the same way. Our passage is a "what" statement, not a "how" statement. It mentions the objective God has established without describing the means He provided in the plan of redemption for its realization. But the context makes it clear that while the problem lies in us—our sin, our ignorance and weakness, our unworthiness—the solution is found in Christ, His atoning blood, His wisdom and power, His merits *(The Great Controversy,* pp. 623, 617f.). Thus she shows that our sin problem can be solved only through the redemptive work of Christ imputed to us by faith.

3. We have seen previously that in the past some have lived so close to God that they would have chosen to die rather than knowingly commit a wrong act. They had reached the condition described in the passage we are considering. Yet they realized that in spite of their

radical commitment and outstanding faithfulness to God, they were as dependent on Christ's merits as any other fallen being. That is why they confessed their sinfulness, recognized their unworthiness, and trusted fully on His redemptive work, imputed to them by faith, for a right standing with God.

4. The experience of the remnant church—the believers still alive during the time of trouble—will be similar to that of God's faithful children in the past. They honestly endeavor to live in harmony with God's will, sincerely repent of their sin, and deliberately refrain from consciously cherishing any sinful desires. And yet they will confess their sinfulness, recognize their unworthiness, and grieve over their shortcomings. That is why they will depend on Christ's redemptive work on their behalf as fully as did all previous believers.

This understanding of the passage we are considering has many significant advantages over the interpretation we mentioned before. First, it allows the passage to speak for itself without either reading into it what is not really there or pushing it beyond its proper limits. Second, it preserves a natural consistency between the passage and its thematic context—discussed previously in the fifth chapter. Third, it harmonizes with the many comments Ellen White makes on this subject elsewhere in her writings—some of which we have discussed throughout this book. Fourth, it avoids the serious problems created by the interpretation that attempts to harmonize it with the perfectionistic views advanced by E. R. Jones and others. And fifth, we can adequately substantiate it from Scripture.

Many Differences, and Yet No Difference

Many differences will exist among the redeemed as

they enter the Golden City. In their lives on earth some of them had been highly educated and were quite familiar with what God has revealed about His plan of redemption. Others had no schooling whatsoever—they had never even heard that there was such a thing as a Bible. Some had been honest, morally irreproachable persons even before they became the adopted sons and daughters of God in Christ. Others had been hardened criminals who had to battle with their evil tendencies and vicious habits all their lives. Some responded to the gospel in repentance and faith long before their cases came for review at the pre-Advent judgment, and consequently made considerable progress in their character development and behavior modification. But others accepted God's reconciling grace at "the eleventh hour" and therefore experienced hardly any changes at all.

These are all real, significant differences. Yet they are all circumstantial, and therefore have no bearing on the eternal destiny of those involved. As far as the ground for their salvation is concerned, the redeemed will all be the same. If God had judged and rewarded them on the basis of who they really were and what they had actually done, then all without exception would have been found guilty before Him. Not one of them would have been worthy of eternal life. But because He treated them on the basis of their response to the salvation He provided in Jesus Christ, they all were made participants with Him of the Father's inheritance.

Because by their repentance they indicated that they recognized their personal inadequacy, and by their faith they indicated that they accepted Christ's redemptive work on their behalf, all the redeemed of all ages are entitled to full sonship through Jesus Christ and are welcome as guests at the wedding feast of the Lamb.

Each of them has a golden crown, the sign of total victory through the atoning blood of Christ. And each of them is dressed in white garments, the symbol of the perfect righteousness of Christ, which gave them access to eternal life. They all know:

> This righteousness from God comes through faith in Jesus Christ to all who believe. There is no difference, for all have sinned and fall short of the glory of God, and are justified freely by his grace through the redemption that came by Christ Jesus. . . . [God] did it to demonstrate his justice at the present time, so as to be just and the one who justifies those who have faith in Jesus (Rom. 3:22-26).

That is why Jesus Christ will be first and foremost to all the redeemed in the earth made new.